PineScript Technical Indicator Development

Copyright © 2022 Minakshi.

All rights reserved. No part of this publication may be reproduced, distributed, or transmitted in any form or by any means, including photocopying, recording, or other electronic or mechanical methods, except in the case of brief quotations embodied in critical reviews and other non-commercial uses permitted by copyright law.

Second Edition 2022.

PREFACE TO FIRST EDITION

One of my Instructors in Harmonic Patterns introduced me to PineScript on the TradingView platform. The instructor demonstrated the uses of the Harmonic tool on Tradingview's charting platform and asked us to submit our assignments as screenshots.

This was the first time I used charting tools on TradingView, and I found them easy to use compared to other charting tools available for free on the internet. After a few months, I realized that this is more than a charting tool. Traders can set alerts and automate their charting using custom indicators, which saves traders much time in manual scanning and tracking of tons of scrip. Further Tradingview allows you to write custom indicator and backtesting scripts using their proprietary sudo-script known as "pinescript". You do not need a particular computer or software to create pinescript; it can be done on any computer with any hardware specification as long as there is internet connectivity and a browser. TradingView is a powerful charting and alert tool with the facility to back-test trading strategies and highly customizable charts.

I have no programming experience and initially struggled to learn this simple PineScript programming. I had to take the help of some of my engineer friends and traders familiar with coding. During my journey to learn this simple yet powerful PineScript, I thought of sharing my learning experience with other traders for their benefit. This book is for non-programmers with no prior coding experience by a non-programmer. This book would surely enable you to make quick codes with simple instructions.

Minakshi
12th March 2022
Trader, Author, and a Self Learner

Contents

PineScript Technical Indicator Development 1
PREFACE TO FIRST EDITION 2
Contents 3
Lesson 1: The TradingView Platform 5
    Getting Started 7
    Exploring charting tools 8
    Applying indicators on the chart 12
    Applying strategies to the chart 14
    Paper trading or live trading through trading view. 16
    Bar replay 17
    Chart properties 17
Lesson 2: Making your first indicator 19
    indicator, strategy, and overlay 20
Lesson 3: Plotting multiple indicators: Saving Subscription 23
    Adding more moving averages to Price Chart 24
    Changing the color of the plot 25
    Adding multiple indicators (3 plus) from the Community Library 28
    Do it yourself 31
Lesson 4: Variables and Built-in Variables 32
    How data is stored in pinescript? 32
    Built-in Variables 33
    Coding using the Concepts learned so far 33
    Type of data 35
    Variables 36
Lesson 5: Operators 38
    Why they are called operators? 38
    Relational Operators 38
    Logical Operators 39
    Coding using the concepts learned so far 39
Lesson 6: Conditional Statements 42
    The "iff" statement 42
    The ? : conditional operator 45
    The "if .... else..." condition 46
    Bar marking when open = high[1] 48
Lesson 7: Drawing Shapes/ text/ Labels on chart 51
    The plotshape & plotchar function 51
    The plotchar function 53
    The label function 54
    Label function inside a conditional block 54
    A label can print variables 56

    Label as debugging tool 58
Lesson 8: Loops - Repeating Task 59
    The "for" Loop 59
    The break Statement 61
    The while loop statement 62
Lesson 9: Setting up Alert 65
    Setting Alert from TradingView Interface 65
    Setting Custom Alert 66
    Engulf Screener through PineScript 68
    Explanation to Screener Code 72
Lesson 10: Functions 75
    Built-in Technical Indicators 76
        Average True Value 76
        Exponential Moving Average 77
        Parabolic SAR 78
        Correlation 79
        The Chande Momentum Oscillator 80
        Center of Gravity 82
        Money Flow Index 83
        Stoch 84
        Bollinger Bands 86
        Williams %R 87
        Keltner Channels 88
        Directional Movement Index 89
        SuperTrend 89
    Other major built-in functions 90
        Pivot high and Pivot lows 90
        The crossover and crossunder function 93
        Barssince 95
        The valuewhen function 96
    User-Defined Functions 98
        Example Marking Doji Pattern 98
    Library 100
        Exporting function from library 100
        Importing function from library 101
Chapter 11 : Coding Auction Failure 103
    Identification of Auction Failure (Method-1) 103
    PineScript Code for Auction Failure(Method-1) 104
    Identification of Auction Failure (Method-2) 106
    PineScript Code for Auction Failure(Method-2) 107

Lesson 1: The TradingView Platform

This lesson is very simple, if you are a trader, you are already familiar with charting tools, and therefore, no explanation for charting tools is required. If you are new, the sections below introduce a few essential charting tools, leaving the rest for you to explore and learn.

You are advised to visit "tradingview.com" and signup for a free account. The account provides all the tools for charting, scripting, and trade setups. On the home page of the tradingview website, type the name of your favourite scrip in the ticker window and hit return for the real-time price graph of a ticker.

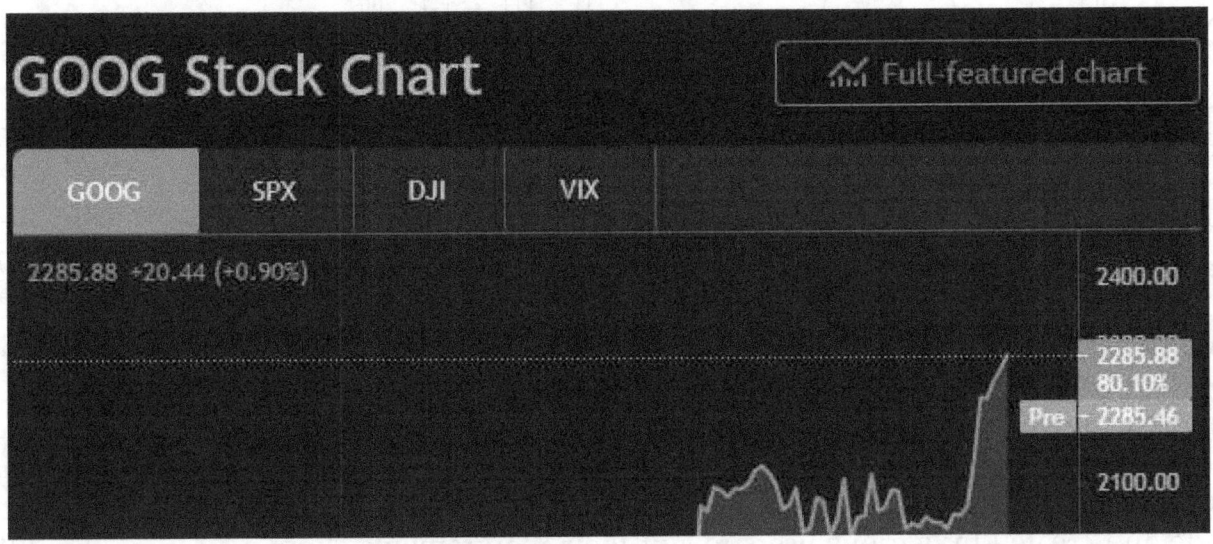

In the interactive chart, you have charting tools on the left panel. These charting tools are similar to any other charting software. If you have worked on investing.com or yahoo finance, you find similar tools to mark a trend, fibo numbers, drawing shapes, etc. On the top panel, apart from the timeframe selection dropbox, you have the "fx" button to add more indicators to the chart. Some are "built-in" indicators like moving averages, RSI, Aroon, accumulation distribution, etc. There is another set of indicators created by users of pinescript and shared for public use; you can call them "community scripts" or "community indicators". You can either select built-in indicators for your analysis or use "user-developed" indicators for examination. It is highly recommended that you use indicators made by other users after careful examination.

Many custom indicators created by users of the TradingView platform are helpful and can be used alone or in combination with your trading strategy. The TradingView platform has provided only a few fundamental indicators, and the rest of the indicators are custom-made and created by various users to suit their requirements. Now, you know how the TradingView platform differs from any other charting tool. The main difference comes from the ability of this platform to share indicators with the community and the features offered by pinescript to create indicators to suit your requirement.

Here is another point that I want to highlight before we proceed further. The free version of the trading view platform does not allow putting multiple indicators on screen. Limiting the number of indicators is done to limit resource consumption on their server. TradingView encourages users to develop a single indicator script by merging multiple indicators into one. You can always bypass many of the limitations imposed by the TradingView platform's free version by coding and allowing multiple indications in your custom indicator, thereby saving an entire subscription.

Getting Started

Below is the first screen you get after signing up with tradingview.

Just search for your favourite ticker ID and hit the search button. Tradingview provides a nice technical chart for the ticker. In the below example, I have opened a well-known ticker.

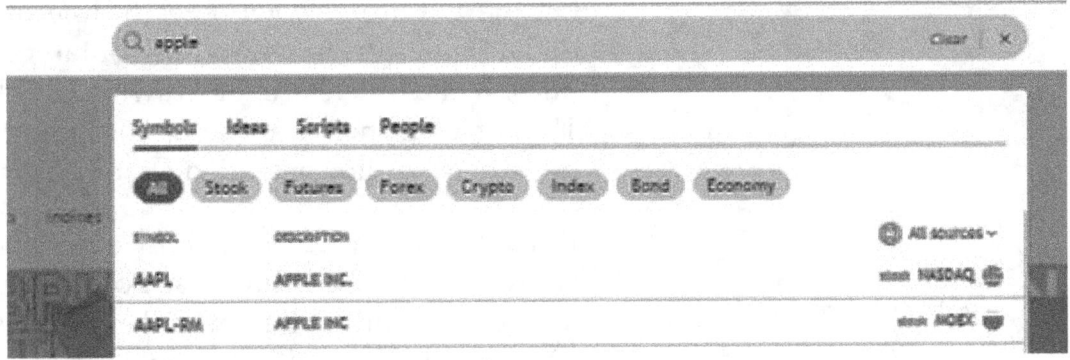

Below is the ticker chart wherein tool icons of the technical charting tools appear on the left of the chart. You are free to explore all the available options on the charting tools. However, in the chapter, we provide a quick overview of the charting tools and some lesser-known features of the trading view platform before we move ahead.

Exploring charting tools

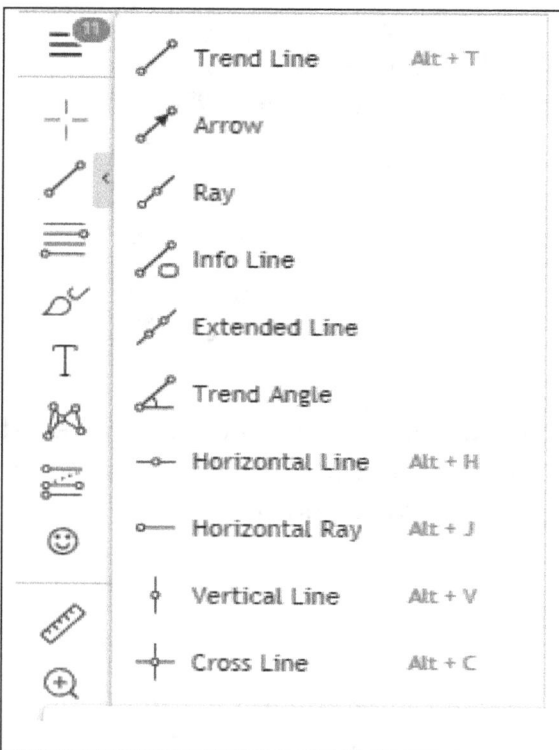

On the left are various types of line drawing tools. Some are to draw horizontal / vertical lines, while others are for drawing trend lines. These trend lines can also be in the form of a ray, arrow, or line extended at both ends.

When I mark a price level, I use a ray line with an extension in one direction. Some Gann fans like to draw lines at a particular angle, say 45 degrees. The line with an angle can be drawn by the trend angle option shown on the left.

Double-click the line drawn or the object drawn on the screen to access more properties of the line or object. Below are the properties of a ray.

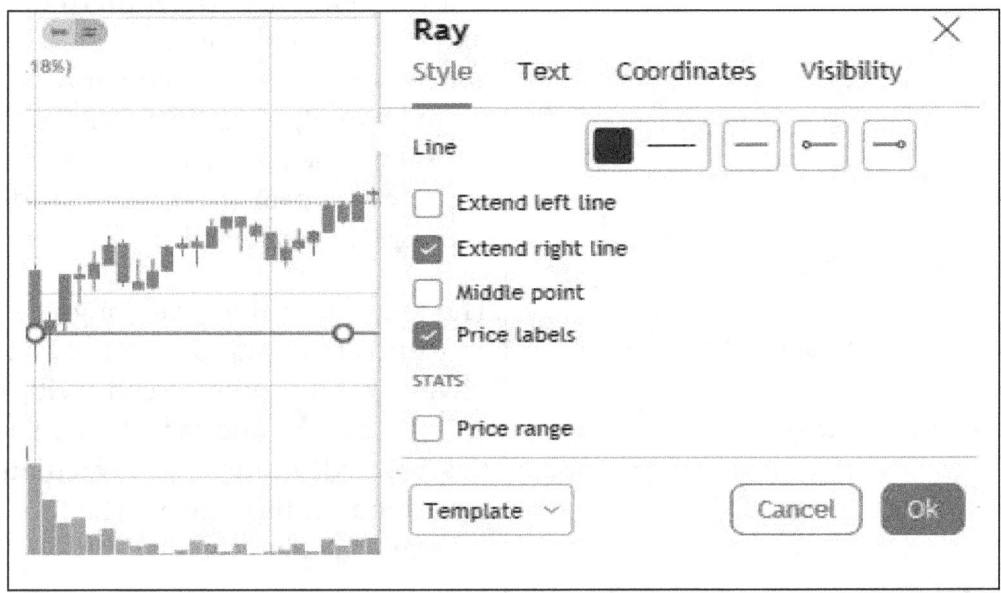

The ray line properties/options can change the line's colour, shape or thickness. The property can be set to display price labels with the line or to extend a line in the left/right direction. There are many other options/properties that you may explore. Similarly, all the charting objects discussed below can be double-clicked to access their properties and can be customized according to needs.

	On the left is an option known as "magnet". This charting option is not available in other charting softwares. This option allows you to select the exact high/ low/open or close of a bar.
	When we mark a bar, say it's high or low, selecting the exact high or low point becomes challenging. The click could be either a few ticks more or less than the exact point. The system automatically selects the nearest open/high/low or close point if this option is enabled. The nearest point is attracted for selection, thus the name magnet. As a harmonic trader, I use it more often than others.

All the options shown on the left of the screen are not generally available in other charting software. The important one is the fixed range volume profile. This option allows you to select two bars and plot the volume on the vertical axis for the bars between them. Many traders use the volume profile for identifying support/resistance or trade opportunities.

The top two options, i.e. long-position and short-position, help calculate the risk-reward ratio on the screen. With this tool, entry, stop loss and target are marked. The risk-reward ratio is calculated and displayed on the screen. The tool can save time on calculations.

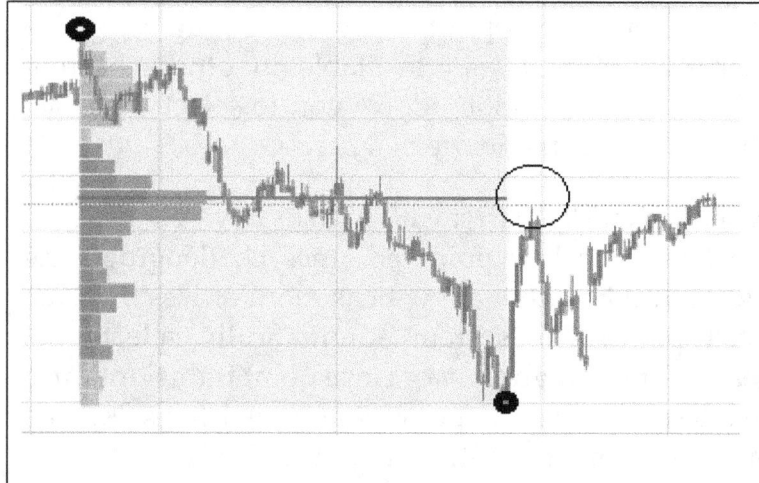

The charting option for the "fixed range volume profile" is on the left. The volume is plotted on the vertical axis when the extreme ends of a trend are selected. The highest volume price range also acted as a resistance/support.

The "fixed range volume profile" is unavailable on other free charting softwares since they require lower time frame data for plotting such profiles.

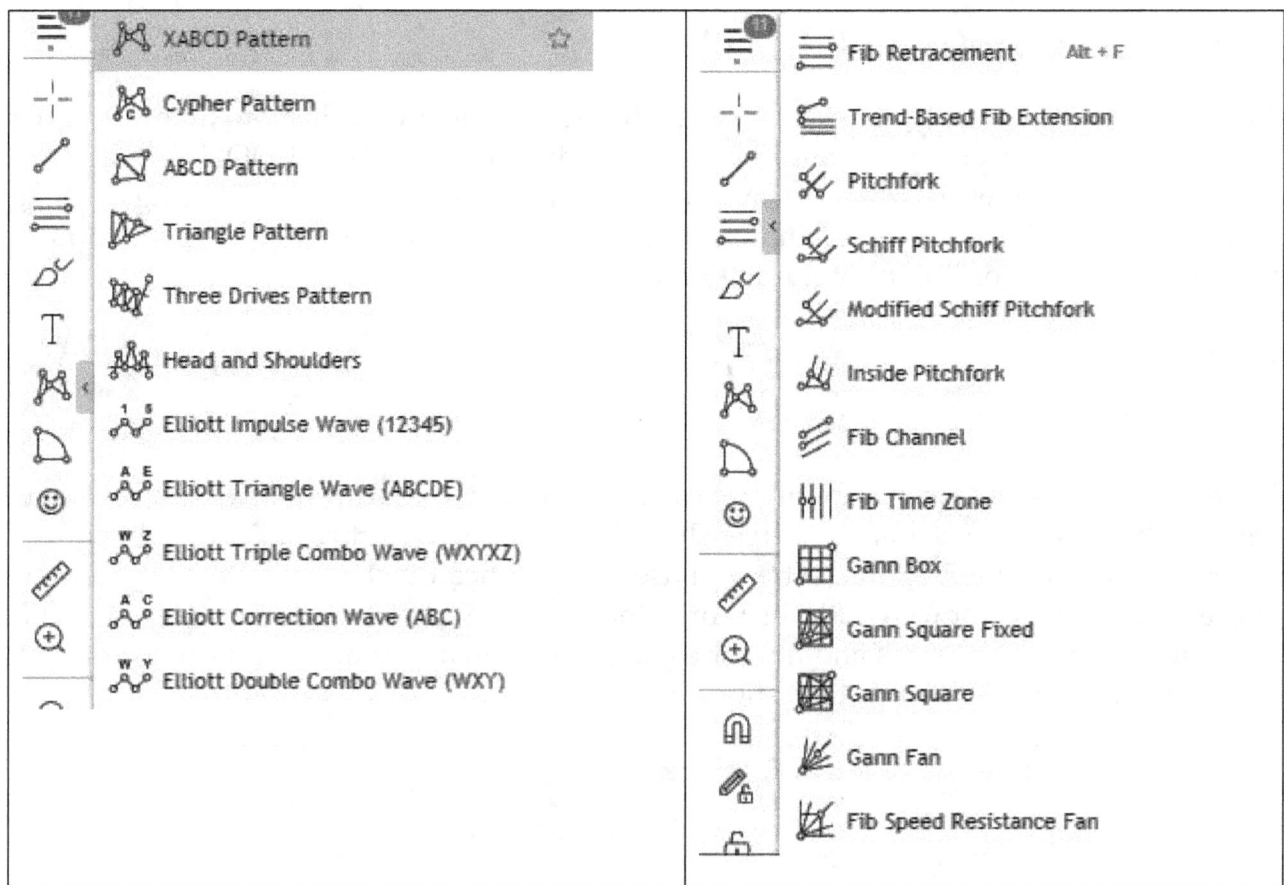

The options on the top left are helpful for harmonic and Elliot wave traders. Harmonic trading involves marking swing highs/lows for the calculation of rations between the respective moves and is analysed in the light of harmonic theory. The above tools are for a separate class of traders and are outside the scope of this book. If you know the harmonic theory, you can use these options for quick marking on the chart and analysis.

Similarly, if you have studied Elliot wave theory, the tools on the left can be used by you for marking the waves on the chart. Apart from harmonic and Elliot options, there are other options for marking and recognising patterns.

On the left are charting options for traders who prefer to use Fibonacci numbers in their trading and use the Gann theory.

Applying indicators on the chart

I firmly believe that the tradingview has the highest number of indicators than any other software in the market. Apart from the regular indicators like RSI, AROON, SMA, EMA, etc, tradingview allows its users to share custom indicators developed for sharing or using by other traders. This feature of sharing indicators by the developers has tremendously added to the indicator library of trading view.

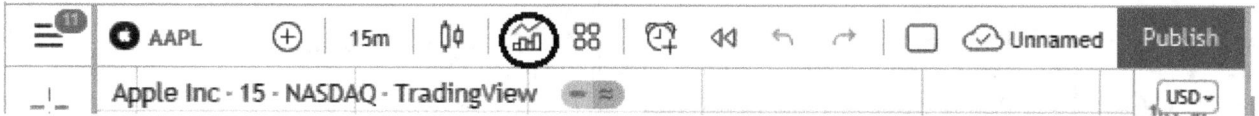

The option to access this indicator library can be found in the charting software's top menu, denoted by a circle in the above screenshot. A single click on this indicator library can increase your excitement. You can try and use many indicators. However, the free version of the trading view allows you to use three indicators on the chart simultaneously. This limitation is only for novices and not for a coder who can apply many indicators through scripts and always bypass this limitation.

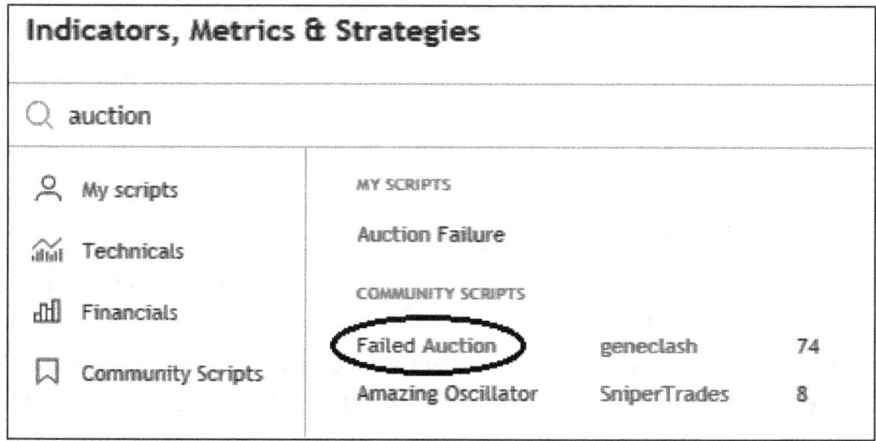

When searching for the "auction" keyword under the indicator section, the script "Failed Auction" by an author "geneclash" under the community script section appears. Search for any other keyword, and you will find that one or the other script relating to your requirement has already been coded by community developers and shared on the pinescript platform for free use. Just double-click the indicator to add the script on your chart as under:

The script added a cross mark on the bar representing auction failure and marked a line of support. The name of the script appears in the top left corner. A mouse over the script's name on the chart provides options like setting or hiding the indicator, viewing its source code, or removing it from the chart.

Do you know what an auction failure is? An auction failure is represented by two consecutive bars having the same high or same low. In the above case, it is precisely same high. Auction failure is covered in the upcoming chapter, where this indicator's code is discussed.

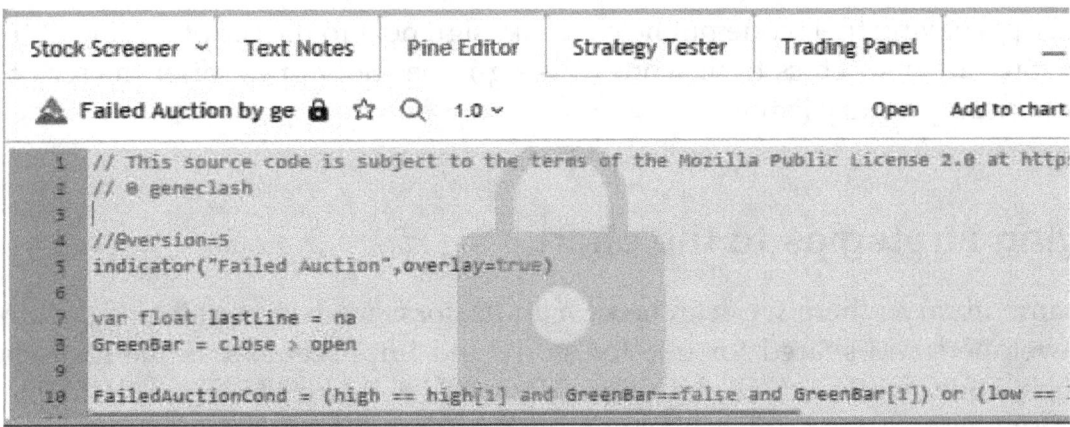

The "{ }" option under the indicator allows viewing the indicator's code in the pine editor window. This code can be reviewed, studied and reused in developing your script as the codes are generally under Mozilla Public License.

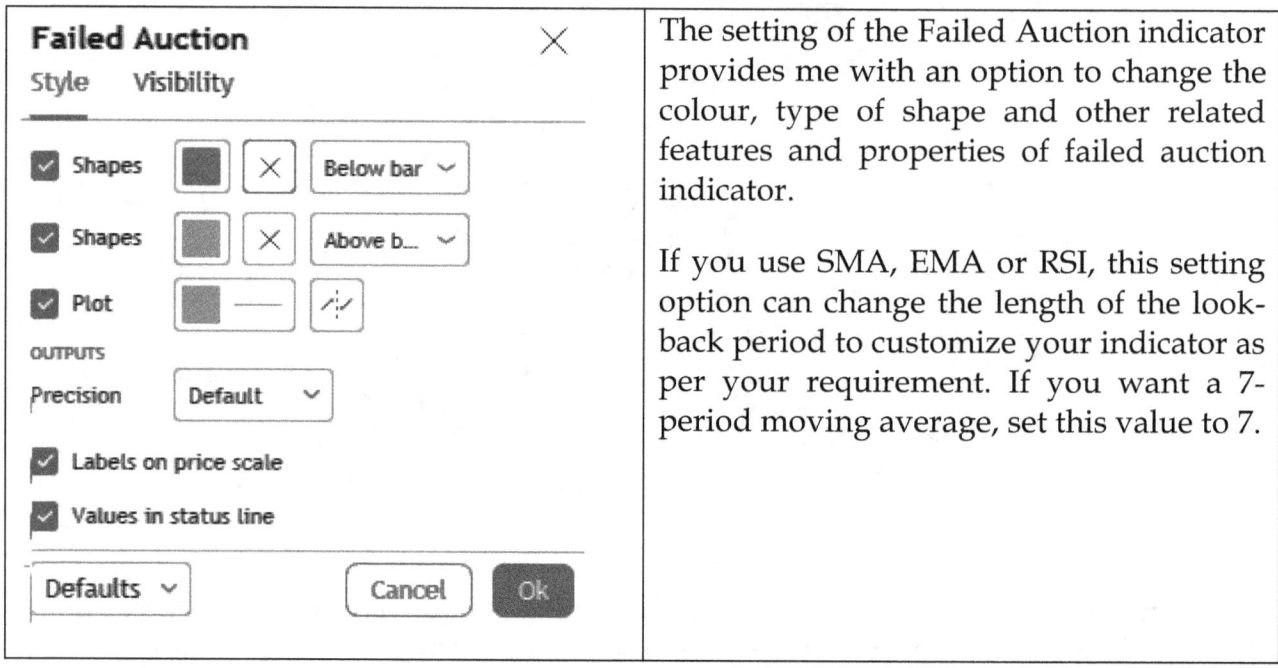

The setting of the Failed Auction indicator provides me with an option to change the colour, type of shape and other related features and properties of failed auction indicator.

If you use SMA, EMA or RSI, this setting option can change the length of the look-back period to customize your indicator as per your requirement. If you want a 7-period moving average, set this value to 7.

While you explore codes by other authors, notice that not all authors allow sharing or viewing of the codes. Some authors allow their scripts to be used by the public, but the code is not made public.

All the scripts having their code public have a { } sign next to the script's name. If the script does not provide free access to the code, this sign does not appear after the script's name in the community library listing.

Applying strategies to the chart

In the same library where we searched for indicators, we have strategies developed by some developers and shared for free for study and improvement. Some may choose to share their code, while others may not. Now let's explore strategies available in the community library.

I searched for some strategies and found one in the library; the above script's code is available for viewing. Clicking the icon next to the source code opens a page with a strategy description provided by the developer. You can identify the strategies in the library by the strategy icon next to the strategy's name, with two arrows pointing to the wave sign. Just click on the script's name to add it to the chart.

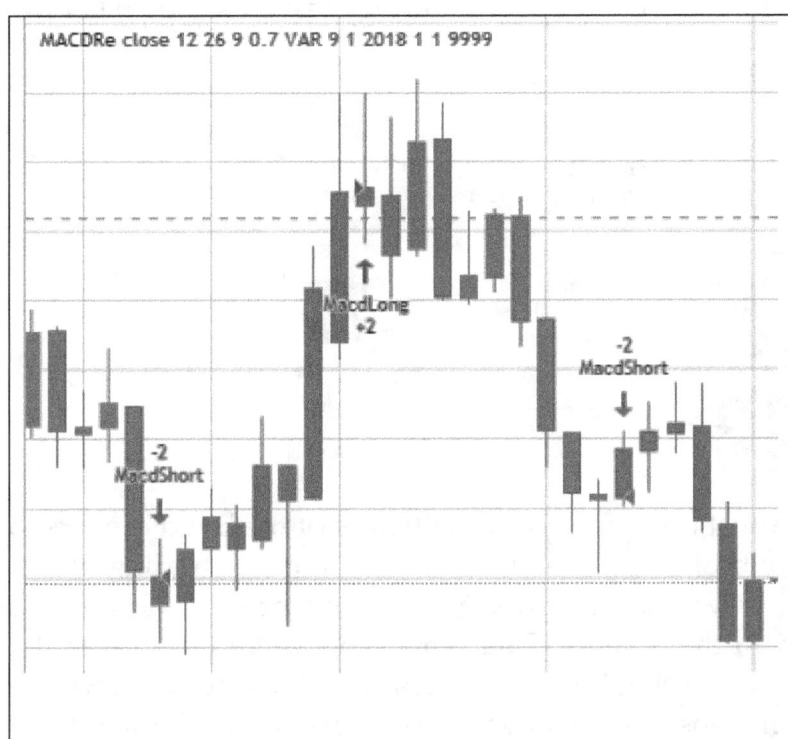

Adding the strategy script to the chart has resulted in appearing of buy-sell signs on the chart. In this case, MacdLong and MacdShort words appear with the entry-exit signs.

The appearance of buy/sell signs means that the strategy is working on the chart. You can examine the buy-sell signals on the chart, or if you are interested in the mathematics of the strategy, i.e. % winning trade, profit per cent, number of short trade or long trade, you have to look below the chart for the button named "strategy tester".

The strategy tester provides a detailed analysis of the strategy along with a graphical representation of the profit-loss matrix. Under the strategy tester, you have two other tabs - performance summary and list of trades.

The above strategy has provided a net negative result. The negative result could be because we are using it on the wrong time frame or ticker than the intended one. Reading the developer's notes before using any strategy is always suggested. For the time being, till we take this topic into detail, I suggest exploring these profit-loss statistics.

Paper trading or live trading through the trading view.

Trading view supports some brokers worldwide, and you can directly place your buy and sell orders from the screen of trading view. Note that the strategies developed in the pinescript are still not allowed to place a buy/sell order on your behalf through the tradingview platform. Placement of direct orders may have some legal issues and, therefore, not enabled. To access the broker or to know supported brokers on the tradingview, just click on the trading panel tab next to the strategy tester as shown below:

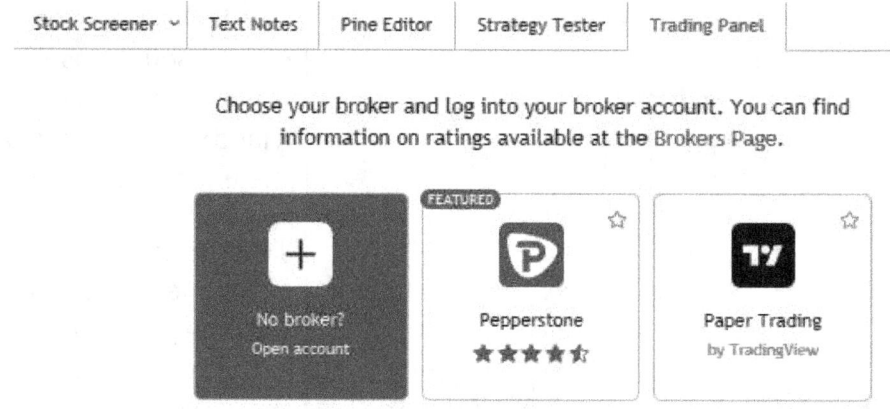

If your broker is not on the list, you must open an account with any of the listed brokers to place an order from tradingview. My broker is not on the list, so I do paper trading. Paper trading is an option in the trading view platform to buy, sell, and practice on the live market on virtual money provided in the account. The remaining section discusses the feature to connect to paper trading and placing buy-sell orders from the screen. However, if you have a broker account, all other steps remain the same; only the broker changes from paper trading to real broker.

To connect to paper trading, click "paper trading", and your account with virtual money will become available for trading.

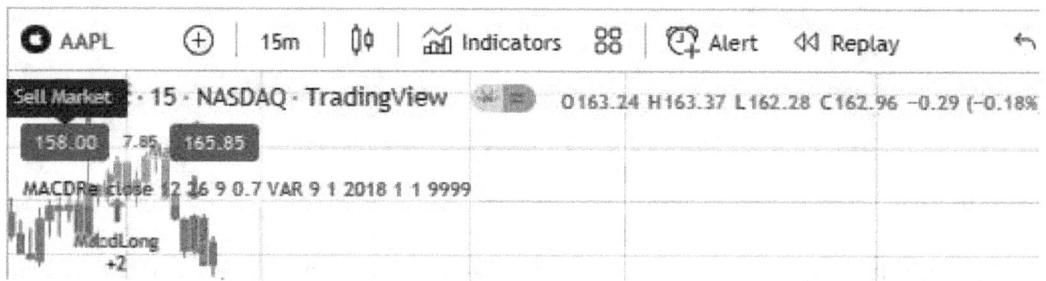

You can place buy-sell orders from the left top corner where buy-sell ask bid prices appear in red and blue. The above screenshot is pre-market; hence the buy-sell prices are not shown correctly. Or you can trade by right-clicking on the chart and selecting the trade.

Bar replay

Bar replay is one of the most exciting features I use when I have nothing to do. Under this feature, generally available to paid users or users with a trial period, historical bars are presented to the user one by one as if the live market is working. All those traders who think they have developed enough trading skills to do trade by intuition can also use this feature to check their abilities.

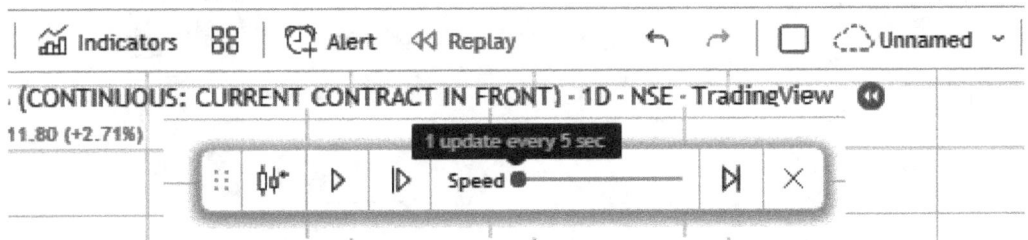

Activate the bar-replay feature by clicking on the "bar-replay button" and selecting any historical bar to make it the initial bar for replay. Now, under the bar replay setting, you can set the time interval for the automatic appearance of each bar or click the next bar button to obtain the next bar. For example, I want to work on 30 mins historical bar automatic replay; then I can set the replay setting to 5 sec for the bar and starting point to start bar replay. Under this option, the following 30-minute bar is presented on the screen every 5 seconds. The only drawback of the automatic replay is that the bars cannot be delayed beyond 5 seconds. If you need more time, manually obtain the next bar by pressing the next button. Bar replay is an excellent feature to practice on historical bars with your trade setups.

Chart properties

The default look of the tradingview charting is a dark theme that I do not like. I like a clean white background with a black bar for the downward closing bar and a hollow for upward moving bars. The global setting for the charting can be done from the chart setting options

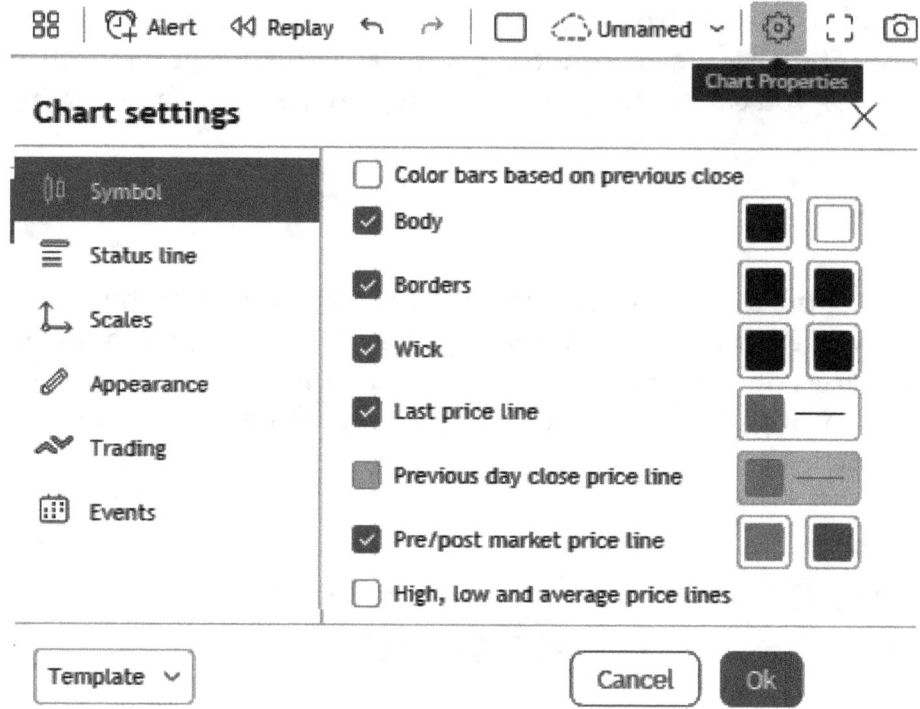

You can explore the chart properties to suit your colour theme. From the next chapter onwards, the focus is more on the pinescript, and I would leave the rest of the work for exploring alerts, watchlists, timeframes, sharing of charts, etc., to you.

Lesson 2: Making your first indicator

I assume you are a trader but lack programming skills to make codes to create and customize indicators. It will be an added advantage if you have prior experience with the Amibroker programming language, i.e. AFL.

In this book, programming skills are taught through coding and creating programs. I will not complicate learning indicators by teaching computer basics irrelevant to pinescript. It will be explained when the need arises to explain a particular part of a code.

You create pinescript code in the pine editor, located below the interactive price chart. The programming language used for making these codes is known as pinescript. PineScript is a trading view-specific programming language created to code only on the trading view platform. The pinescript language cannot be used on other platforms. However, learning pinescript allows you to use concepts in other programming languages.

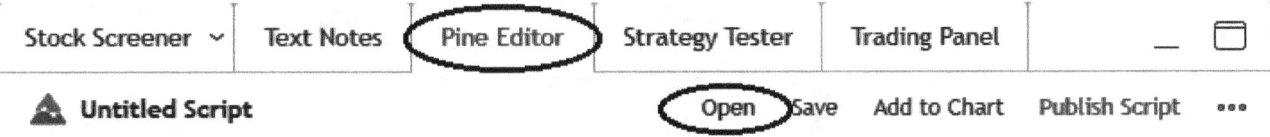

After clicking pine editor, click on the open button and select "new blank indicator"

```
//@version=5
indicator("My Script")
plot(close)
```

The button opens a new blank indicator in the editor window. The above code is automatically generated. The above code is for plotting close values on the chart. Let's save this code first by the name "script01". You can save the code by clicking the save button next to the open button shown in the above screenshot. Once the code is saved, click on the "add to chart" button. This "add to chart" button is next to the save button. The "add to chart" executes the script by plotting close values on the screen. The result is shown in the below screenshot.

Congratulations ! you have made your first program, and the result is on your screen. The close value is shown in a separate window below the original price chart. Now, is this helpful? I think "no"; the price should have been plotted on the chart, not below it. We need to make some corrections to the code to make it appear on the price chart. Here, we learned our first pinescript code.

indicator, strategy, and overlay

The "overlay" keyword is a type of instruction to change the behaviour of a chart. The "overlay" tells the chart's location to Tradingview, where we want to draw the indicator. The "overlay" can take two values, one is "true", and another is "false". If "overlay" is set to "true", the graph is plotted on the price chart, and if it's "false", the chart is drawn below the chart.

Let's see where this instruction code should be put in the "script01" we just created. Line number one should be as I have written, i.e. "//@version=5". This line lets the system know we want to use version 5 of the script.

```
//@version=5
indicator("My Script",overlay=true)
plot(close)
```

The instruction goes under the bracket after the indicator. The "indicator" is another keyword that you should remember. The "indicator" keyword tells the trading view that we are creating an indicator, not a strategy. It would have been "strategy" if you were creating a strategy. So the first word after "//@version=5" will either be "indicator" or "strategy". Since we are now learning "how to make indicators?" this first word will be "indicator".

Inside the bracket after the indicator keyword, we can define a set of values to customize the indicator's behaviour. i.e. whether to plot below or above the chart, etc. All such behaviour aspects are written inside the bracket after "indicator". The first one under the bracket is "My Script"; this is the name of the script, also known as "title" you can change it to your name or "PlotClose" or anything you want.

In the first code, i.e. "script01", we had not defined overlay=false; still, the chart is below the price chart. Why?

We take an example. Let's say you go to a new city and need a hotel for the night. You will ask the hotel manager about the room rent. You expect that if you are taking a room in a hotel, the bed with mattresses would be there. You further expect TV, carpet, toilets, etc. Probably you would not ask for the availability of these things from the hotel manager. If you have some special requirements, you would tell only those requirements to the manager, like internet connectivity, room service for dinner or lunch, blue coloured carpet etc.

Similarly, when you have stated that you want to create a new indicator. The instruction creates a structure of indicator that is generally used. If you want, you can change the indicator's behaviour, which can be done under the indicator's bracket. Otherwise, without any special instruction, the indicator is created with standard specifications. The special instruction inside the bracket separated by commas are known as parameters.

Now onwards, I will name each script and refer to them by 'script' name.

Let's run the "script02" as under :

```
//@version=5
indicator("script02",overlay=true)
plot(close)
```

Before you save and run this script, you are advised to delete the earlier plot from the screen by clicking the remove button, as shown in the image below.

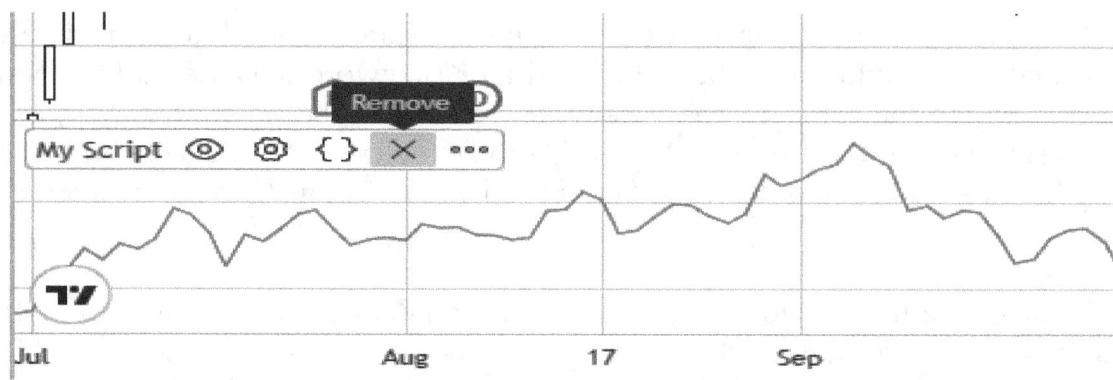

Now save the revised script and again add it to the chart. The indicator now works. The output of the script is shown under :

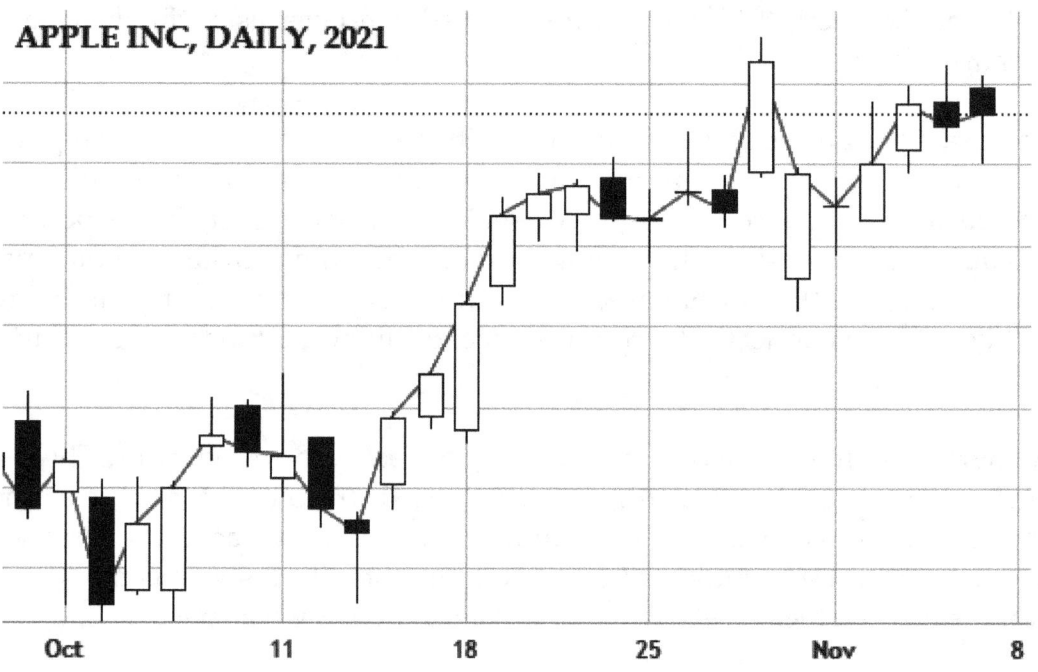

Each of the close values is now plotted on the chart by connecting the close of each candle.

We can also write indicator code as under :

indicator(title = "script02",overlay=true)

Both have the same result. However, this code clarifies that "script02" is the script's name and the value of overlay is true. Both title and overlay are known as "parameters" of the indicator function.

Lesson 3: Plotting multiple indicators: Saving Subscription

Some authors claim that their book or article can save you a subscription to trading view. They further claim that the cheat codes in the book allow multiple indicators on the chart. It's not a cheat code or a hack. The makers of the tradingview platform encourage coders to use scripts to customise their indicators. By using custom indicators, you can use any indicators or parts of the indicator per your requirement.

Here in this lesson, we plot an SMA, i.e. simple moving average and then try to add multiple moving averages on the chart.

```
//@version=5
indicator("script03",overlay=true)
plot(ta.sma(close,14))
```

The above code can plot a simple moving average(S.M.A.) for 14 bars calculated on the close value of each bar. The only difference from the earlier code is that now instead of "close" inside the plot, we have ta.sma(close,14)".

We have already studied the code 'indicator("script03", overlay = true)'. The 'indicator' instructs the system that we are making an indicator, and it has the name "script03" and has to be plotted on the price chart and not below the price chart.

Last time we used "plot" to plot the "close" value on the chart by use of plot(close). Now in place of close, we have written ta.sma(close, 14) to plot S.M.A. for 14 periods. Now, here are several questions that may arise in your mind. I try to solve them one by one.

1. It's cumbersome!
   Yes, we can make it more simple by changing the code and making it more readable as

   ```
   //@version=5
   indicator("script03",overlay=true)
   sma14 = ta.sma(close,14)
   plot(sma14)
   ```

   We have stored the moving average value for 14-bars calculated on close in sma14. Then we plotted the sma14 as we had plotted 'close values' in the last script.

2. What is this "ta.sma(close,14)"? How do I get this for calculating the moving average? Pinescript provides certain built-in functions (built-in functions are shortcuts to long calculations). Built-in functions reduce your coding job.

Functions can be assumed as a black box, you only need to provide input, and the function provides results. You need not bother about the calculations. PineSciptt has various built-in functions to reduce your work. Built-in functions are discussed in upcoming lessons.

For now, assume functions as a black box that takes inputs through the brackets. Inputs are written inside the brackets and are separated by commas. For example, the "SMA" function takes two inputs (parameters) inside brackets but is separated by commas. These inputs are written inside a bracket after the "ta.sma" keyword. The "ta" before "sma" stands for "technical indicator", and "sma" means "simple moving average".

Adding more moving averages to Price Chart

A very simple trading strategy is a cross-over of moving averages. In this strategy, you have two moving averages with different periods (14 periods and 7 periods). A buy signal is generated when a faster-moving average(say 7 periods) crossovers with the slower one (say 14 periods). When the faster-moving average crossunder the slow-moving average, a sell signal is generated.

Intending to visualize two moving crossovers, I have already plotted 14 bars moving average, now plot another moving average with a different period, say 7 bars on the same chart. The 7-bars moving average can be created by adding another set of code in "script03" as under :

```
//@version=5
indicator("script04",overlay=true)
sma14 = ta.sma(close,14)
sma07 = ta.sma(close,7)
plot(sma14)
plot(sma07)
```

We have already discussed the calculation of the moving average and its plot. In the above code, "script04", we have added another set of moving averages by repeating the code for calculating moving averages and plotting them. The only difference is that now the period is 7 instead of 14. The result produced by the script is shown below:

Congratulations! You have plotted two moving averages on the chart with a single script. How do you feel about the above plot? Are they good enough to work? In my opinion, it's good, but I cannot distinguish between the 14-bar and 7-bar moving averages because the colour of the plot lines is the same. They should have been different. The plot function uses the default colour parameter of blue colour; therefore, both lines are blue.

Changing the colour of the plot

How can you change the plotline? Is it a property or behaviour of an indicator or plot? The plot is the result of the "plot" instruction; therefore, to change the behaviour of the plot, other parameters (inputs) are added to the plot.

It is the same as explained in my previous example, you go to a hotel and ask for a room. Now you need to explain to the hotel manager that I need two beds, one with a blue blanket and another with a red blanket. Without instruction, the hotel manager would provide both beds with standard specifications.

Similarly, in the absence of any instruction to the plot, the plotline of the following specification would be created:

1. A "normal thickness" denoted by 1
2. "Continuous line" with "blue" colour

You can provide additional instructions to the "plot" to change colour, thickness, or line style. The following are major offerings in the form of parameters by the "plot" function of pinescript :

1. **color**: it can be aqua black, silver, grey, white, maroon, red, purple, fuchsia, green, lime, olive, yellow, navy, blue, teal, or orange. You can define the line's colour by just putting a comma followed by "color=color.[name of colour]".

    For a red colour line, I can use plot(sma07,color=color.red) and for a green line, I can use plot(sma14, color=color.green). You can also use hex colours in addition to the above colours. If you are not aware of hex colour codes, just leave it. The above colours already defined by pinescript are sufficient for all practical purposes.

2. **linewidth**: You can also change the thickness of the line by adding another instruction to the plot by putting a comma and adding "linewidth =2"

Although there are many other parameters like style, offset, etc., the details of other parameters at this juncture may confuse you. You can learn more about other parameters when we study other types of drawing tools.

I have added some instructions to earlier "script04" to change line width and colour as under :

```
//@version=5
indicator("script05",overlay=true)
sma14 = ta.sma(close,14)
sma07 = ta.sma(close,7)
plot(sma14,color=color.green,linewidth=1)
plot(sma07,color=color.red,linewidth=3)
```

The result of the code is as under :

The lines are in different colours, and the width of the line has changed. Colour change may not be visible in the book; however, linewidth change is visible.

You must be thinking that I was quick enough to learn all these things as a new trader. I must tell you that you need not learn all the things that we just discussed. The hints and help are already there in the pinescript editor.

```
5   plot(sma14,color=color.green,linewidth=2)
6   plot(sma07,color=color.red,linewidth=2)
7
```

plot (Built-in annotation function)

Plots a series of data on the chart.

Syntax
plot(series, title, color, linewidth, style, trackprice, transp, histbase, offset) → plot

Returns
A plot object, that can be used in {@fun fill}

Ctrl + click (PC) or cmd + click (Mac) on keyword for more help

Put your cursor over the plot instruction in the pinescript editor, and the editor helps you with hints. If you are still unable to understand, you can always press the Ctrl button (cmd button in case of mac) and click on "plot" or whatever keyword you fail to understand to get more details about it.

You can see that the hint provides a syntax detail. Syntax is a structured method of giving instructions. In the case of the plot, it says series, title, color, linewidth, style, track price, transp, and many more.

The series is the list of values that you want to plot. In our case, it was sma07 or sma14. The title is the name you want to give to the line. If you wish, call it title="myLine" or title="sma07" or any name. If you don't give a name, pinescript automatically assigns a random name. We have already discussed colour and linewidth. To avoid complexity in the initial learning phase, I am not discussing other parameters like transp (transparency), offset, style, etc. These parameters can be changed for a plot to customise its looks. The remaining parameters of line functions are covered in upcoming chapters.

Adding multiple indicators (more than 3) from the Community Library

Until now, you have understood that some indicators are plotted on the chart and some below. Some of the indicators are available from pinescript, and some of the indicators are available in the community library. Further, you also understand that the free account at trading view does not allow adding more than three indicators on the chart. Some of the books or articles, or blogs claim that they can provide you with a trick to bypass this limitation of three indicators. There is no trick or hack to bypass the three-indicator limit. The developers of the pinescript encourage users to use pinescript. Using the script, you can combine many indicators in one single script. When the script with combined scripts is added to the chart, it counts as one indicator, not multiple.

We added multiple moving averages on the chart through coding in the previous examples. In this section, we add a community indicator with our developed indicator.

A single script can only have one indicator function; therefore, it can have either overlay = true or overlay = false. You can combine multiple indicators of one type, i.e. the ones plotted on the chart or those plotted below the chart in a single script. You cannot have scripts plotted on a chart or below the chart in a single script – for example, you cannot have RSI and a simple moving average as a single script.

Let's combine the script of the Bollinger band with the failed auction script we found in the community library.

Both scripts are presented below :

```
//@version=5
indicator("MyBB",overlay=true)
[bb1,bb2,bb3]=ta.bb(close,21,2)
plot(bb1)
plot(bb2)
plot(bb3)
```

```
//@version=5
indicator("Failed Auction",overlay=true)

var float lastLine = na
GreenBar = close > open

FailedAuctionCond = (high == high[1] and GreenBar==false and GreenBar[1]) or (low ==
low[1] and GreenBar and GreenBar[1]==false)

if FailedAuctionCond
    lastLine := if not GreenBar
        high
    else
        low

plotshape(FailedAuctionCond and
GreenBar,style=shape.xcross,location=location.belowbar,color=color.green)
plotshape(FailedAuctionCond and
GreenBar==false,style=shape.xcross,location=location.abovebar,color=color.red)

plot(lastLine==lastLine[1]?lastLine:na,style=plot.style_linebr,color=color.red)

alertcondition(FailedAuctionCond,"FailedAuction","FailedAuction!!!")
```

The failed auction script has been obtained from the script's source code by clicking the source code button denoted by { } appearing next to the setting button of the script.

Now since both scripts have the overlay=true, these scripts can be combined. Note that only one name for an indicator function is allowed; therefore, I renamed the indicator name and copy-pasted the code of another script to the bottom of the first script, as shown below:

```
//@version=5
indicator("Combined",overlay=true)

var float lastLine = na
```

```
GreenBar = close > open

FailedAuctionCond = (high == high[1] and GreenBar==false and GreenBar[1]) or (low ==
low[1] and GreenBar and GreenBar[1]==false)

if FailedAuctionCond
    lastLine := if not GreenBar
        high
    else
        low

plotshape(FailedAuctionCond and
GreenBar,style=shape.xcross,location=location.belowbar,color=color.green)
plotshape(FailedAuctionCond and
GreenBar==false,style=shape.xcross,location=location.abovebar,color=color.red)

plot(lastLine==lastLine[1]?lastLine:na,style=plot.style_linebr,color=color.red)

alertcondition(FailedAuctionCond,"FailedAuction","FailedAuction!!!")

[bb1,bb2,bb3]=ta.bb(close,21,2)
plot(bb1)
plot(bb2)
plot(bb3)
```

The portion of the bb script copied in the auction script and other changes in the script's name is highlighted above. Add this script to your code, and here is the output:

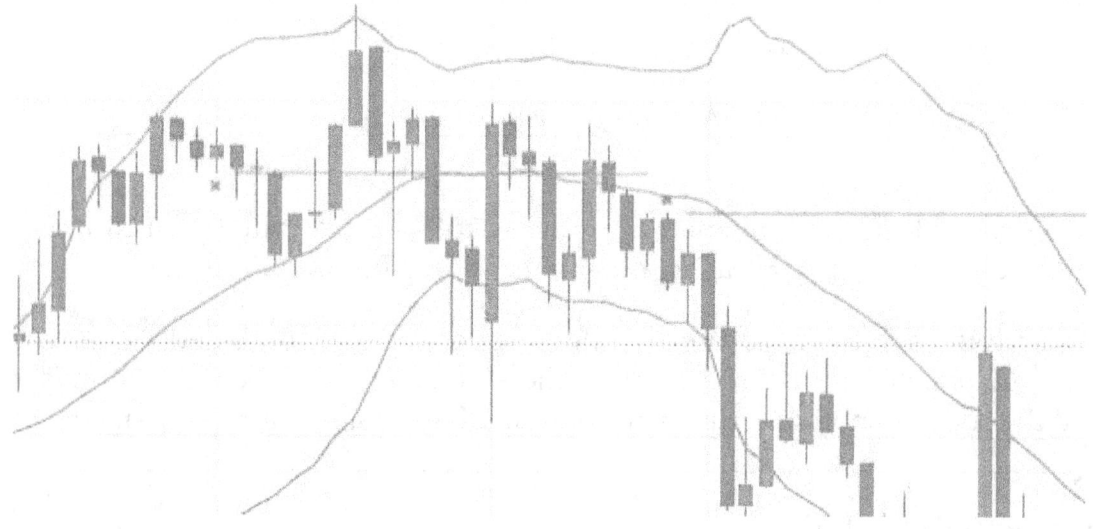

In the above script, I have auction failure and Bollinger band. Observe that no extra coding was done; only one code is copy-pasted below the code of another script after removing the indicator function.

Although the trick provided above will work in all cases, in some cases, when the container name, i.e. the variable name appearing in one script, is identical in another, this would only work after resolving the variable name conflict.

Do it yourself

Another parameter for the plot is style. You can try different styles for a line as an assignment. The supported line styles are the plot.style_line, plot.style_stepline, plot.style_histogram, plot.style_cross, plot.style_area, plot.style_columns, plot.style_circles.

As the name suggests, it changes the way the line is plotted. An example of a step line is shown below:

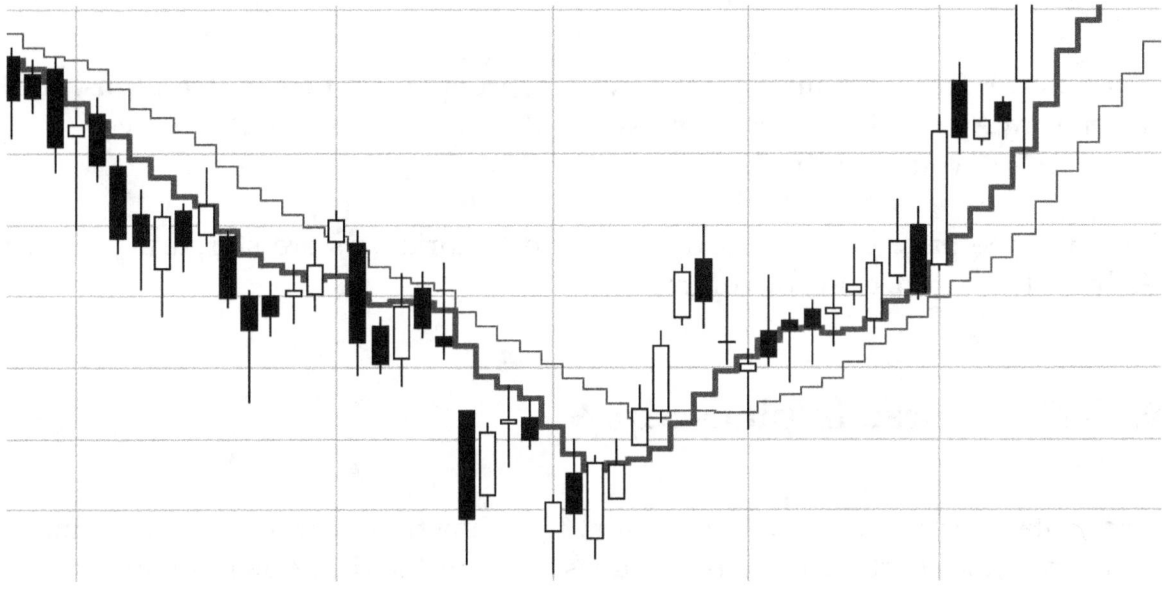

You can add a parameter to the plot function as style= plot.style_histogram to change how the plot is shown on the chart. Please note that the plot.style_histogram is not in quote marks. We will discuss in upcoming sections when to use quotes and when quotes are not required.

Lesson 4: Variables and Built-in Variables

For any technical analysis, you need data. We go to investing.com, yahoo finance, or google finance to get market data. Without this data, you won't be able to do your analysis.

The pinescript provides primary data like open, high, low, close, and volume for scrips in which you are interested. These data can be accessed on pine script by simply using these words. The data, as we know, are stored in a computer's or server's memories. You cannot access data from the memory unless you know the address. It is like your friend lives in the city of New York, and you want to make contact with him. Either you need his home address or phone number to contact him.

Similarly, much data is stored in the system. For easy remembrance of data, you can provide the name of that data. Assume my age is 42, and I want to store this data. I can assign a name to this data. I can call this "age" or can be called as "myAge". I can save my age data by assigning it to that name like :

myAge = 42

Now, whenever I ask for myAge, the system provide 42. In simpler terms, it starts considering myAge as 42. If I ask "myAge > 40", the answer would be "yes". If I ask "myAge < 40", it would say "no".

In pinescript, the price data for current bar and historic bars are stored in the variable named high, low, open, close, or volume.

How is data stored in pinescript?

The price data for scrip are stored in a 1-min, 1-hrs timeframe, or day/weekly timeframe. You can access the chart for these timeframes through the dropdown menu provided at the top of the chart.

The data for each timeframe is stored as a list. For example, the close data would be stored in the form of the following:

100.0	101.5	102.5	99.0	99.5	98.5	96.0	97.5	98.0	99.5
Bar 0	Bar 1	Bar 2	Bar 3	Bar 4	Bar 5	Bar 6	Bar 7	Bar 8	Bar 9

If you want to get the value of close data for the recently closed bar, you can access it by "close".

The "close" value in the above case is 100.0. If you want the historical price of close, i.e. data before the current bar, I can use square brackets like "[ ]" after close and the number of the bar before the current bar inside the square bracket.
The value of close[1] would be 101.5, and close[5] would be 98.5.

The name used to store data is known as variables. They are called variables because they act as containers to store data and can be emptied and refilled with other data. If your age is 42, you can save data as myAge = 42, and if your age changes to 43, you can change the value of myAge by myAge:=43.

If you are reassigning a new value to a variable, you must use the ":=" sign to re-assign a new value to the variable.

Built-in Variables

Some variables are used by pinescript, so you cannot use them to store your custom data. These are open, high, low, close, and volume. These variables are called built-in variables as they already store vital data relating to the scrip.

If you try to save your age as close = 42 or close:= 42, the system generates an error. These keywords are reserved for pinescript. Similarly, there are many other keywords that you cannot use as variables for storing your data.

Coding using the Concepts learned so far

In this section, we calculate a simple moving average for a seven-period without using the function "sma". The moving average is calculated by ourselves without the help of the already defined function "ta.sma". I assume you already know how to calculate an average.

If you want to calculate an average of the bar's close prices for the last seven periods, then you must add the close prices of the seven periods and divide this sum by 7 to obtain your result.

You can do this in excel as under :

Close price	sum	average
1046		
1022		
1023		
1034		
1036		
1038		
1042	7241	1034.429
1002	7197	1028.143
1038	7213	1030.429
1001	7191	1027.286
1047	7204	1029.143
1050	7218	1031.143
1037	7217	1031
1024	7199	1028.429
1042	7239	1034.143

In excel, we can either use formulas directly. However, it is calculated manually by adding the prices for the last seven periods and then dividing it by seven.

To arrive at the first sum and average, I have added 1046+1022+1023+1034+1036+1038+1042 = 7241

You can notice that I have included the current completed bar's value, i.e. 1042.

In pinescript, the value of close for the most recent bar is close, the bar previous to the recent bar is close[1], and so on.

For calculating the sum of the recent close price and the last six close prices in pinescript, we can use

close + close[1]+ close[2]+ close[3]+ close[4]+ close[5]+ close[6]

The complete code for calculating the moving average is shown below:

```
//@version=5
indicator("script06",overlay=true)
sum = close + close[1] + close[2]+ close[3]+ close[4]+ close[5]+ close[6]
sma07 = sum/7
plot(sma07,color=color.red,linewidth=2)
```

Add the above code to any chart, and you get a thick red line representing a simple moving average for seven periods.

In the above "script06" code, we have calculated the sum of close values and stored it in the "sum" variable. Historical values of the close were accessed using [ ] brackets.

Further, note that variable names are case-sensitive. The "Close" is not the same as "close". The names of all inbuilt variables are in lowercase. In coding, camelCase is used for the naming of variables. It is simple if you want to name a variable as "it is my variable", you should capitalize the first alphabet of each word except for the first word. It can thus be named "itIsMyVariable". The camelCase naming is just a convention; no issue if you don't follow these naming guidelines.

Type of data

Data or, in simpler terms, information can be of many types. It can be open, high, low, or close. All such information has values and also has decimal parts. Example: open may have a value of 99.35 or 99.00; they always have values in decimal values. Such types of data are known as float. i.e. any information that may have decimal and numeric parts.

The volume or number of students in a class cannot be expressed in decimals. They are always in whole numbers and do not have decimal parts. You can never have 34.5 students in your class. It could be either 34 or 35. Such types of data are known as integers.

Other types of information, like the name of the scrip, i.e. "apple" or "goog" or your name, are of English alphabets and are known as "words" or "strings". In coding, they are generally put inside single or double quotes. Example: study(title="script01"). Here, "script01" is a name or a string; therefore, it is enclosed inside a single or a double quote.

Sometimes, information is stored as "yes" or "no". Such types of data that can only store information in the form of "true" or "false" are known as Boolean-type data. Is open > close, the answer could only be in the form of "True" or "False". No other form of answer is possible.

Apart from the above four basic data types i.e.

1. Integer
2. Float
3. String
4. Boolean

In pinescript, we have various other data types like date, color, style, etc. To define such color, style, etc we have constants to represent them. In the last lesson, we studied some of them in plot function.

Variables

I have already introduced variables to you in previous sections. You can define variables as names given to memory locations where your data/information is saved. These memory locations have technical names like "00AAX0"; to make them more coder friendly, we give them names. We can call "00AAX0" as "Joe". Whenever I call Joe, this memory location provides me with data.

Depending on data types, i.e. integer, float, or string, variables can also be of these types.

In pinescript or any other programming language, you cannot store one data type along with another data type. For example, if you have a variable myAge to store your age in the whole number, i.e. integers, then you cannot store float values in myAge. This is because "myAge" has not reserved or planned enough space to store the decimal part of the float. After all, it was initially planned to store integers; therefore, it only has space to store an integer.

The following example would clear this concept :

myAge = 42

myAge := 42.5

The above generates an error. Why?

In the first line, we have assigned the whole number 42 to the "myAge" variable. Whenever you assign a variable the first time with a "=" sign, the variable becomes equal to the value on the right side of "=" and adapts the data type. i.e. the variable creates a memory structure to store the value of that data type. However, in the following line, we have asked the system to reassign the value 42.5 to myAge. Now, since myAge has already created a memory space to store only whole numbers, it does not have the facility to store decimal parts of the number and, therefore, generates an error. This problem can be corrected by the following:

myAge=42.0

myAge := 42.5

In the first line, we have asked the system to store 42.0 in the "myAge" variable. Now, the myAge variable reserves memory space in the system to store numbers with their decimal parts. When asked system to reassign 42.5 to the variable "myAge", it does it happily.

Sometimes you may require to convert one data into another data type. For example, you want to convert age into a string to print "My age is 42". We know that you cannot store one data type with another. Here, "My age is" is a string, and to convert 42, an integer, into a string, you may use the function tostring(myAge). We will be using these functions in upcoming lessons.

As of now, you may note that converting one data type into another is possible, and this process of converting is known as type casting.

Lesson 5: Operators

We can find all types of fancy definitions of operators on the internet. For simple understanding, note that plus, minus, multiplication, divide, etc., are all operators. These signs are placed between two numbers or expressions. Depending on the sign between the numbers or expressions, they are evaluated. If a plus sign is placed between two numbers, they are added, and if the sign is negative, the difference is calculated.

Why are they called operators?

They are called operators because they perform operations between two numbers. The sign of the operator is placed between these two numbers.

Example: 4 + 5; here, we have a plus operator, and the operation is performed between 4 and 5.

You already know the basic four operators that we just discussed, and you also know how they work. They are called arithmetic operators. Now, I come to other operators

Relational Operators

The list of relational operators is given below:

Relational operators (>, <, ==, =!, >=,<=)	Example	Result
> (greater than)	5 > 4	True
> (greater than)	4 > 5	False
< (less than)	5 < 4	False
< (less than)	4 < 5	True
== (equal to, comparison)	5==4+1	True
== (equal to, comparisons)	5==4-1	False
=! (not equal to)	5=!4+1	False
=! (not equal to)	5=!4-1	True
>= (greater than or equal to)	5>=4+1	True

<= (less than or equal to)	5<=4+1	True

In the above table, I have provided a list of all the relational operators, examples, and results. The result provided by relational operators is always in the form of "true" or "false". i.e. Boolean type.

The relational operators compare two numbers, two variables, or one number/ string with a variable. You can note that the data type on either side of the relational operator should be the same for its functioning. You cannot compare Amelie with 12. Both should be integers or strings for a relational operator to function.

Logical Operators

The list of logical operators is given below in the table.

AND	Compares two Boolean values; if both are "true", the result produced by the AND logical operator is also "true". Example: engulfing= high>high[1] and low > low[1]; if the present high is higher than the previous high and the present low is lower than the previous low, the value of engulfing would be "true" else "false".
OR	Compares two Boolean values; if any one of the two is "true", the result produced by the OR logical operator is also "true".
NOT	It works on a single Boolean operator. It reverses the result of a boolean value. If the boolean value is "false", putting the NOT operator makes the result "true", and if it is "true", it makes it "false".

Coding using the concepts learned so far

In this section, a simple code to dynamically change the colour of the plot line is presented. The script of the earlier lesson is modified here.

```
//@version=5
indicator("script07",overlay=true)
sum = close + close[1] + close[2]+ close[3]+ close[4]+ close[5]+ close[6]
sma07 = sum/7
```

```
myColor = sma07 > close?color.green:color.red
plot(sma07,color=myColor,linewidth=2)
```

Here, we have stored the value of the sum of the close prices for the last 7 bars in a variable named "sum". Further, the "sma07" variable stores the average value for 7 bars.

We have used a conditional ternary operator, i.e. "?" for the conditional value assignment in the "myColor" variable. The syntax of this ternary operator can be defined as :

```
Result_variable = logical condition? result when true: result when false
```

If the value of sma07 is above close, the colour in the "myColor" variable becomes green, else red.

If you are working on version 4 or below, you can also use the function "iff". The function "iff" has been removed in version 5 of pinescript. This function is similar to the excel function "if" that you may have used in excel.

The syntax (format to instruct system) can be defined as :

```
Result_variable = iff(logical condition, result when true, result when false)
```

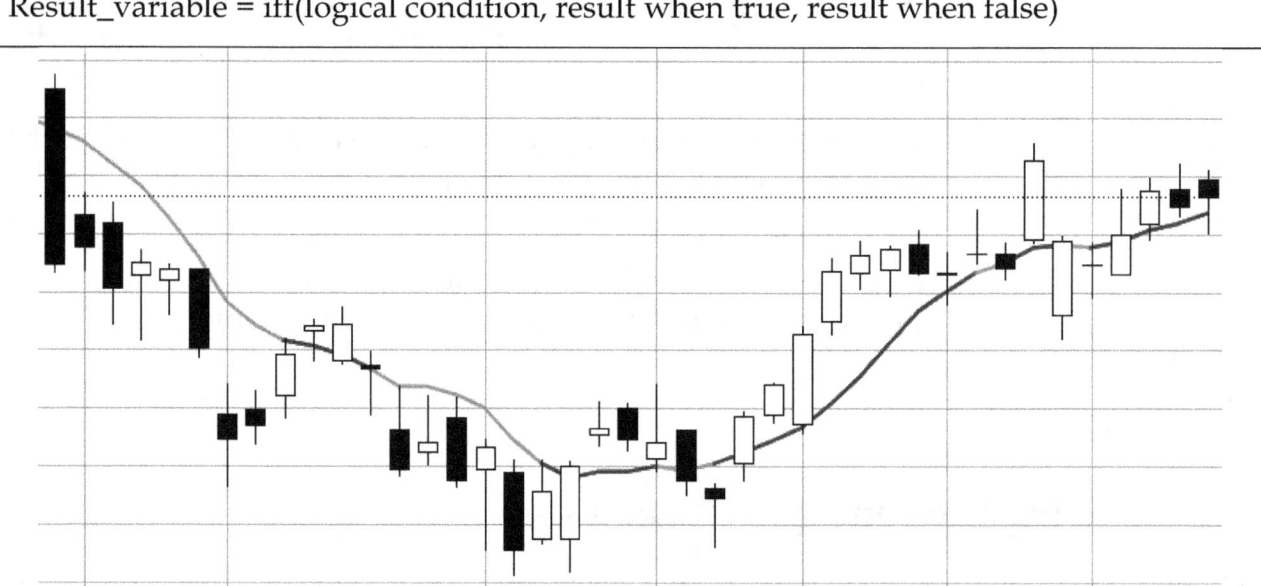

The "iff" function takes three inputs separated by commas. The first one is the logical condition provided immediately after the start bracket of "iff". Suppose the logical condition is "true". In that case, the result_variable takes the value provided immediately after the logical condition. If the logical condition is false, the result variable takes the third input near the close bracket as its value.

The result of script07 is provided in the above chart. The line's colour changes to green if the close is below the line or turns red if the bar's close is above the seven-bar moving average. The colour may not be visible in the book, but there could be a change in the shade of the line in a greyscale book.

Now, I re-explain the code for clarity:

myColor = iff(sma07 > close,color.green,color.red)
If sma07, i.e. moving average calculated, is above the current bar's close, the value of "myColor" becomes color.green, else it is color.red

The variable "myColor" now stores the value of color. This variable is now assigned to the "color" parameter of the "plot" function to do dynamic colouring of the line. Change colour constants to have desired value of colour.

Take another example, myResult = iff(marks > 40,"pass","fail")

If the value of marks is above 40, the value "pass" is stored in the variable myResult; else value "fail" is stored in the myResult variable.

If you are working on the pinescript code of the older version, i.e. version 4 or below, you should charge all the codes with "iff" by ternary operator "?" as explained above to use them in version 5.

Lesson 6: Conditional Statements

We have already come across two conditional statements in the last script, i.e. "iff" and "?". Conditional statements are used to execute certain statements on the logical condition being true and to execute another set of statements on the logical condition being false.

In computer programming, instructions are executed from top to bottom in sequence. i.e. one line by line from top to bottom. However, conditional statements can be used to branch the execution of instructions. Branching is done to provide more flexibility as per the requirement.

Let's take an example for marking all those bars that have open=close[1]. For this, the program would run in a sequence like

1. Check the close of the previous bar. Is it almost equal to the open of the current bar?
2. If the condition at 1 is true, then mark the bar
3. If the condition is false, do nothing

If the condition is "false", the instructions for marking the bar are skipped. Skipping of some statements can only be done through conditional statements.

The "iff" and "?" statement used in the earlier example is generally used for the assignment of value; however, if you need to execute multiple statements, you have to use the "if....else... " conditional statement.

The "iff" statement

The "iff" statement is no longer used in version 5 of pinescript; however, it is vital to understand the "iff" statement if you would like to work with codes of other programmers who have created a script in version 4 or below. The "iff" statement is similar to excel's "if" statement, as explained in the previous chapter. An example of excel is shown on the next page for quick reference.

In excel, an example is shown, if the student's marks are more than 40, she is "pass" or else "fail". The formula is shown above in the formula window of excel.

Here we have used an "if" statement and have compared the marks with 40; if the marks are less than 40, the excel cell takes the value "fail", else "pass" value is stored in the excel cell.

		f_x	=IF(B2<40,"fail","pass")

	A	B	C	D
1	Roll no	Marks	Result	
2	21	46	pass	
3	22	85	pass	
4	23	23	fail	
5	24	8	fail	
6	25	66	pass	
7	26	58	pass	

Similar to excel, we have an "iff" statement in pinescript. If the condition is "true", the value next to the condition is stored in the variable, else the third value is stored in the variable.

Here, you can notice the following :

1. The "iff" statement can execute only one statement.
2. The "iff" statement is used for the assignment of value to a variable
3. The "iff" statement requires the type of two alternative variables provided after conditions to be of the same data type.

Some examples :

```
resultVariable = iff(high > 500.0, high,500)
```

The above statement is wrong because the data type of high and 500 are not identical. The high is a float, while 500 is an integer. They both should have the same data type.

```
resultVariable = iff(high > 500, high,500.0)
```

Again the above statement could be wrong because, in comparison, high, a float data type is compared with an integer data type, i.e. 500. To make 500 a float variable, add a decimal and a zero after that, i.e. 500.0.

The "iff" statement can also be used in a nested form, i.e. multiple "iff" statements inside one another can be used. An excel example is shown below:

```
=IF(B2<40,"fail",IF(B2<50,"Grade C",IF(B2<60,"Grade B","Grade A")))
```

	A	B	C	D	E	F
1	Roll no	Marks	Result			
2	21	56	Grade B			
3	22	97	Grade A			
4	23	38	fail			
5	24	42	Grade C			
6	25	33	fail			
7	26	12	fail			

Here in the example, if the marks of a student are less than 40, she is failing, and if the marks are between 40-50, she gets "Grade C", and if marks are between 51-60, she gets "Grade B" else she gets "Grade A".

A pinescript implementation of the above code could be as under :

```
resultGrade=iff(marks<40,"fail",iff(marks<50,"Grade C",iff(marks<60,"Grade B",
    "Grade A")))
```

The above implementation assumes that students' marks are stored in a series-variable named "marks" and are integer type only.

I take another realistic example, where I would like to classify volume depending on volume activity. Volume classification is typically done under VSA (volume spread analysis), wherein high-volume bars and low-volume bars are required to be identified frequently.

I classify volume into five categories and assign category "5" if the volume is meagre and "1" if the volume is very high.

```
00: //@version=4
00: study("version4 script")
01: volAvg = sma(volume, 40)
02: V = volume
03: volpos =  iff(V>(volAvg*2),1,iff(V>(volAvg*1.3),2,iff(V>volAvg,3,iff(V<volAvg and
        (V<volAvg*0.7),4,5))))
04: //1 = veryhigh, 2 = High, 3 = AboveAverage, 4 = volAvg //LessthanAverage, 5 =
lowVolume
```

Note that the above code is incomplete and written in version 4, not version 5; it is just like a snippet. Here at line 01, the average volume of the last 40 periods is calculated and stored in the variable volAvg. On line no 2, volume is assigned to V; the assignment to V is done to make it more readable on the subsequent line, which is very long.

On line no 3, the "volpos" is a variable that stores the classification value of the volume. The meaning of each classification value is defined in the commented line no 4.

The above is an example of a nested "iff" statement; wherein a value is assigned if the condition is true, and on the condition being false further condition is evaluated for proper assignment to a variable. A typical structure of an "iff" nested statement would be as under :

> iff(condition, [value when true],iff(condition,[value when true],……

The ? : conditional operator

The above conditional operator is similar to the "iff" conditional statement we have just discussed. The ternary operator is available in version 5. You have to change all the code statements written in the "iff" style into this format to run them in version 5. This is also used for conditional assignment and can also be used in nested form.

The syntax of the conditional operator denoted by "?" is as under:

> resultValue = condition? value_on_true:value_on_false

The last example is again repeated with a conditional statement wherein if marks are greater than 40, a "pass" value is stored, and on marks being less than 40, a "fail" value is stored

> resultValue = marks > 40?"pass":"fail"

Due to more reliability of the "iff" statement, I preferred to use "iff" statements in version 4 in place of the "?" operator for the assignment. However, in version 5 "iff" statement has been removed, and it is generally accepted that the "?" statement is faster in execution as compared to the "iff" statement. This function is discussed over here so that in case you come across any script that uses the "iff" operator; you are not taken by surprise. The "?" operator can also be used in nested form. An example is shown below:

> resultGrade=marks<40?"fail":marks<50?"Grade C": marks<60?"Grade B":
>   "Grade A"

In the above example, you can note that no brackets have been used as we had used in the "iff" statement; therefore readability of the code is poor.

The "if .... else..." condition

Just like the previous conditional statement, this statement also evaluates a condition, and on being "true", a set of statements is executed, and another set of statements can be executed on being false. The significant difference between the "if...else" and "iff" statements are as under :

1. The "if...else" can be used for the value assignment or the execution of other statements, whereas the "iff" statement can only be used for the assignment of values.
2. The "if...else" statements can execute multiple statements, whereas the 'iff" can only execute a single statement. Overall, the "if ....else" statement is more powerful and can provide more flexibility to your code.

The general syntax of the "if....else" statement is as under :

```
If [condition]
    Statement no 1
    Statement no 2
    Statement no 3
else if [optional conditional block]
    Statement no 1
    Statement no 2
    Statement no 3
```

The earlier question of "pass" and "fail" grading of students implemented in excel and also with pinescript's "iff" statement can also be implemented in "if...else" style as under :

```
if marks < 40
    resultVariable = "fail"
else
....resultVariable = "pass"
```

The earlier question of grading marks for students can also be implemented in this "if...else" style of code.

```
if marks < 40
    resultVariable ="fail"
else if marks < 50
    resultVariable ="Grade C"
else if marks < 60
    resultVariable ="Grade B"
else
```

```
resultVariable ="Grade A"
```

The code, when written in "if...else" style, has more readable than nested "iff" or ternary operator - "?". The code is straightforward to understand, and I feel no further explanation is required on the above code.

I want to clarify some points with you before we move forward.

1. The "else if" statement is optional and used for nested "if...else". We have used "else if" in the second program for grading and not in the first program for marking fail or pass.

2. The "else" statement is optional and can be completely avoided if you don't need it. An example is shown below for your understanding:

```
if marks < 40
    resultVariable ="fail"
if marks < 50 and marks > 40
    resultVariable ="Grade C"
if marks < 60 and marks > 50
    resultVariable ="Grade B"
if marks > 60
    resultVariable ="Grade A"
```

3. The "if...else" statements can execute multiple statements, as shown below:

```
volAvg = ta.sma(volume, 40)
volpos = 0
if volume > volAvg*1.5
    volpos :=1
    barColor = color.blue
if volume < volAvg * 0.3
    volpos:=5
    barColor = color.red
```

The above example is similar to the grading. In this code, volume classification according to the volume activity is done. Colours have been defined according to volume classification. High-activity bar colour is blue, whereas the low-activity bar colour is red.

Note that the above code is incomplete and is here for illustration purposes only. The colour of the bar assigned in such codes must be used while plotting bars on a chart to complete this code.

In the above example, we have executed two statements simultaneously.

4. The indentation of code is very important in pinescript. When the "if" block code is executed, the system does not know up to which point codes must be executed after a condition becomes true. As a rule, four spaces or a tab space is provided as indentation, i.e. before the code statement, to make them a single code block.

5. In the above example, wherein two statements are executed after the condition is true, note that 4 spaces are provided before the two statements that are required to be executed after the "if" condition becomes true.

Sometimes, the statement of code may be very long and not fit in a single line, so you may have to continue the code to the next line. In case of continuing code on the following line, you may have to provide non-standard indentation, i.e. space less or more than 4 spaces, to let the system know that the statement is continuing from the previous line. An example is shown below :

```
00: //version = 4
00: study("version4 script")
01: volAvg = sma(volume, 40)
02: V = volume
03: volpos =  iff(V>(volAvg*2),1, iff(V>(volAvg*1.3),2,
       iff(V>volAvg,3, iff(V<volAvg and (V<volAvg*0.7),4,5))))
04: //1 = veryhigh, 2 = High, 3 = AboveAverage, 4  = volAvg   //5 = lowVolume
```

The instruction code on line number 3 is very long. Therefore, the instruction is split into two lines. However, on the next line, an indentation, i.e. leading space before the code statement, is provided. This space is 3 spaces, i.e. non-standard indentation to let the system know that the statement from the previous line is continuing on this line.

Bar marking when open = high[1]

The buy or sell decision based on open=high[1] is a common strategy many traders follow. According to this strategy, a short position is taken when the opening is equal to high.

Below is the source code for identifying open = high of the previous bar.

```
//@version=5
indicator("script07",overlay=true)
if open < high[1]*1.002 and open > high[1]*(1-.002)
    label.new(bar_index,high,xloc=xloc.bar_index,text="O=H")
```

The above script is for marking the bar when open of the current bar is equal to the high of the previous bar. In practicality, the current bar open cannot be the same as the closing of a previous bar.

For example, assume the last day's equity high was 25.10; if the current opening is 25.05 or 25.15, can it be considered open equal to the previous day's high? We may need to have some flexibility in terms of tolerance for values.

In the script07 code, the line below incorporates that flexibility.

```
if open < high[1]*1.002 and open > high[1]*(1-.002)
```

I have assumed a tolerance value of 0.2%. If the opening is either less by 0.2% or more by 0.2% from the last high price, the condition will become "true", and the following statement for the marking bar is executed.

The next statement under the "if" statement block is for marking a bar that we will cover in the next lesson.

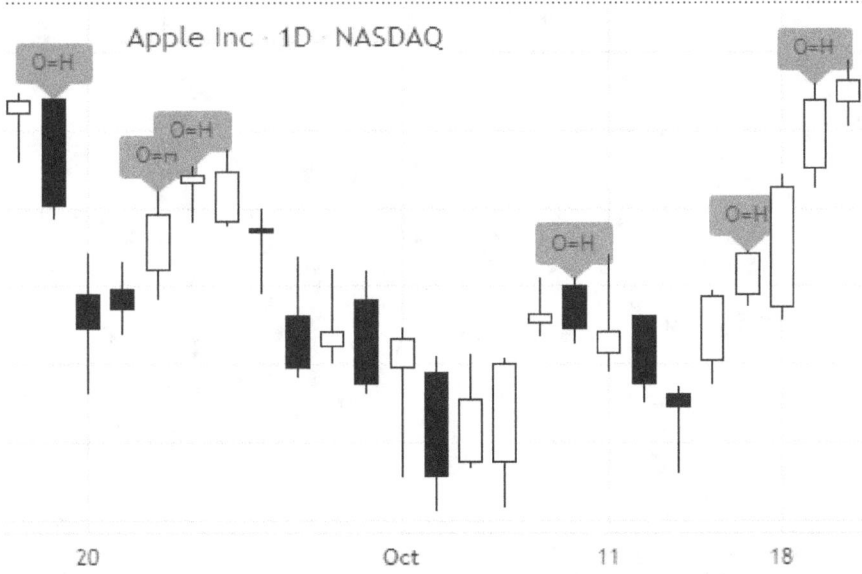

The output of script07, when added to apple inc on Feb 2021, is shown above. It has marked all bars that have "open" almost equal to the high of the previous bar. You can always change the tolerance value if you want.

You can notice here that a short position on all the bars where open is equal to high cannot be undertaken; we may need some additional filters to make the best decision.

Similar to the open = high scanner we just created, another code can be created for scanning and marking the bar when open is almost equal to low. In such cases, traders enter into a long position after verifying other indicators.

The code is provided below for implementation :

```
//@version=5
indicator("script08",overlay=true)
if open < low[1]*1.002 and open > low[1]*(1-.002)
    label.new(bar_index,high,xloc=xloc.bar_index,text="O=L")
```

The label.new function will be discussed in the next lesson.

Lesson 7: Drawing Shapes/ text / Labels on chart

Many times you may have to mark bars on a chart. In our last example, we had marked open = high and open = low bars on the chart. For marking bars on a chart, pinescript has some built-in functions. In the last example, we had already used "label" for marking. We cover all such bar-marking functions in this lesson and shall also discuss their differences.

The plotshape & plotchar function

Pinescript provides an inbuilt function for marking a circle, cross, or other shapes above or below the bar. As already studied, inbuilt functions can take input from users and customize the output per requirement.

The plotshape requires only one input for plotting shape on the chart, i.e. a series with yes/no value.

Below is the code for identifying the bar engulfing the previous bar.

```
//@version=5
indicator("Engulf",overlay=true)
plotshape(high>high[1] and low< low[1])
```

The output of the above code on the "Apple Inc" daily chart for Oct 2021 is as under :

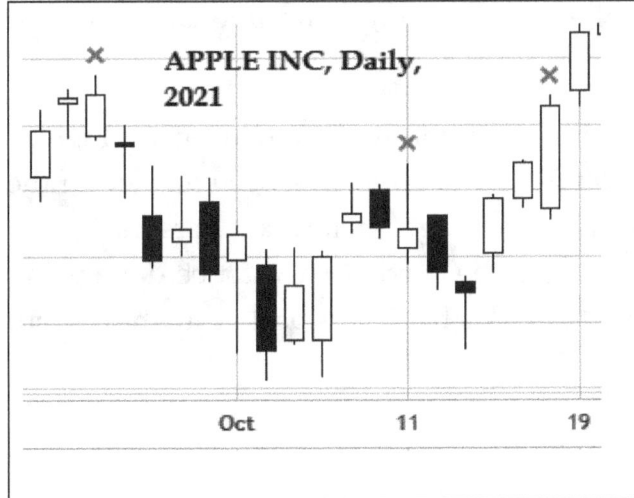

The plotshape has plotted a mark with the following specification:

Colour = blue

Shape = cross

Location = above bar

As we have learned in the previous lessons, these are default offerings of the built-in function, and you can request for change in some or any of the behaviours by providing additional parameters.

The options are available in plotshape for colour, location, and shape customization.

1. Colour: In previous lessons, we learned about the available colour codes. There are some built-in colour constants like color.red, color.blue, etc., and you can also define the hex-code colour. If you want to change the shape's colour, you need to pass an additional parameter inside the bracket of the function after a comma. For example, if you want to change colour to red, you can add color=color.red

2. Location: The location possibility offered by the plotshape function is location.abovebar, location.belowbar, location.top, location.bottom, location.absolute. I have mostly used location.abovebar and location.belowbar. You can try other types of locations by making suitable changes to the code. For example, if you want to change location to below the bar, you can add location=location.belowbar

3. Shapes: The shapes that can be plotted under plotshape are shape.xcross, shape.cross, shape.triangleup, shape.triangledown, shape.flag, shape.circle, shape.arrowup, shape.arrowdown, shape.labelup, shape.labeldown, shape.square, shape.diamond. The default shape that is on the chart is shape.xcross. You can try other types of shapes by making suitable changes to the code. For example, if you want to plot a diamond shape, you can add style= shape.diamond.

Apart from the above most common feature changes that can be done, plotshape offers additional features like

1. <u>Additional text remarks</u>: Additional remarks can be added to the plotshape. The text remark is printed above the shape of the chart. For example, if you want to add a remark as "engulfing", you can do the same by using an additional parameter, text="engulfing"

2. <u>Shifting marking a few bars forth or back</u>: If you want to mark pivot high or low, these pivots only become known after 2-3 more bars have been formed in the opposite direction. You can then mark the pivot high or low 2-3 bars back. The marking of a bar which is some bars back from the current bar, can be done using parameter offset. For example, if you want to mark a bar 2 bars back from the current bar, you can use an additional parameter offset=-2.

This is one of the example for its implementation

```
plotshape(high>high[1] and low< low[1], title="MyEngulfing",
style=shape.diamond, location=location.belowbar, color=color.red, offset=-1,
text="engulfing", textcolor=color.blue)
```

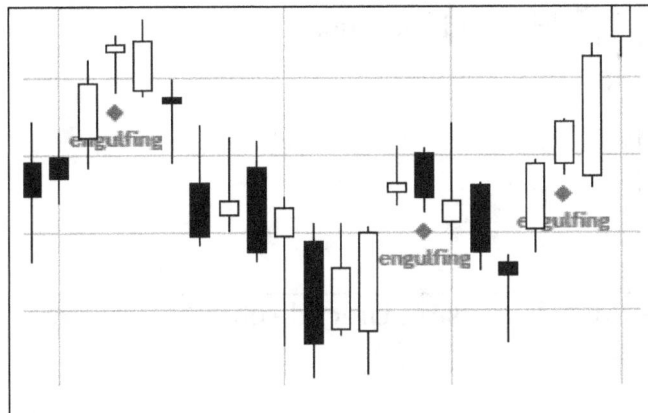

The output generated is shown on the left.

There are some more parameters for further customization of a plotshape. You can also refer pinescript manual by pressing the control button and clicking plotshape in the editor window.

The plotchar function

The plotchar function is used to print a character on a chart. You may argue that the same can also be done with the plotshape function. Yes! I agree that most things can be done with the plotshape function, but the only additional benefit of using a plotchar function is that it supports ASCII and UNICODE symbols. We first look at the syntax with major parameters before taking an example.

```
plotchar(series, title, char, location, color, textcolor, offset, text)
```

In place of a series of Boolean, you can also provide a condition. All other parameters are similar to the plotshape function discussed in the previous section. The only new parameter that it offers is "char".

```
//@version=5
indicator("My Script",overlay=true)
plotchar(open < high[1]*1.002 and open > high[1]*(1-.002),char="§",text="plotchar")
```

The above is code for plotting a Unicode char on a chart; you can also plot your text.

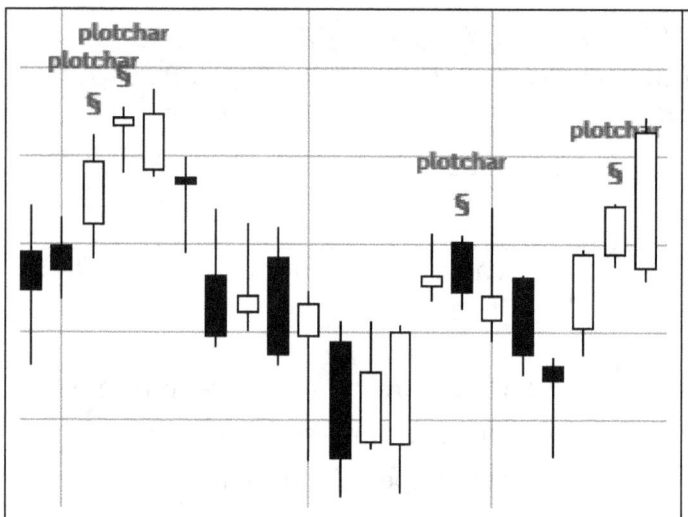

Here in the output, the text's colour is the default. The "drawchar" can set different colours for char and text. You can explore the syntax for a better understanding of function. I leave it up to you to learn about other parameters and their uses.

Can you print bear faces or snowflakes on a chart using Unicode char?

The label function

I consider marking labels the most important and powerful function of the above three functions for marking bars. The significant advantage of the label function over other functions are as under :

1 . The label function can be used inside conditional blocks and loops, whereas plotshape and plotchar functions cannot be used inside a conditional block such as "if …else".

2. The variables can be converted into strings and printed on the chart using a label function, whereas you can only print a constant string using plotshape and plotchar.

3. The functionality defined in s.no. 2 above for the label function can also be used for debugging pinescript.

Now for your better understanding, I will provide examples of the above.

Label function inside a conditional block

In the previous example, for marking open=high, we used a label inside a conditional block. The code is again reproduced here for ready reference

```
//@version=5
indicator("script07",overlay=true)
if open < high[1]*1.002 and open > high[1]*(1-.002)
```

```
label.new(bar_index,high,xloc=xloc.bar_index,text="O=H")
```

Let's now use the plotshape function for marking a cross mark above the bar on condition for the open being equal to the high of the previous bar. The code is presented below:

```
1  //@version=5
2  indicator("Open Equal High",overlay=true)
3  OEH = false
4  if open < high[1]*1.002 and open > high[1]*(1-.002)
5      OEH:=true
6      plotshape(OEH,style=shape.xcross,location=
7          location.abovebar,color=color.blue)
```

```
Add to Chart operation failed, reason: line 6: Cannot
use 'plotshape' in local scope.
```

The plotshape function requires a series of Boolean as its first input. When a new series OEH is set to "true" when the condition for open equal to high[1] is true, the system throws an error showing that plotshape cannot be used in a local scope.

The error can be corrected as under :

```
01: //@version=5
02: indicator("script08",overlay=true)
03: plotshape(open < high[1]*1.002 and open > high[1]*
04:   (1-.002),style=shape.xcross,location=location.abovebar,color=color.blue)
```

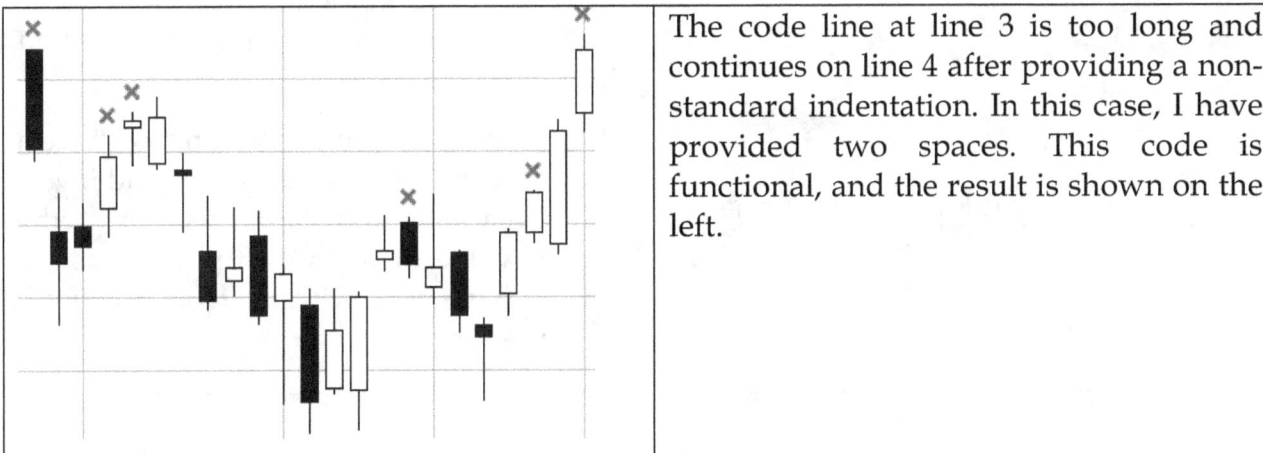

The code line at line 3 is too long and continues on line 4 after providing a non-standard indentation. In this case, I have provided two spaces. This code is functional, and the result is shown on the left.

The plotshape, since having first input as the condition itself, the creators of the pinescript felt that it would be unnecessary to allow plotshape inside if …else block or any loop blocks. We will be coming to loop blocks in upcoming lessons.

A label can print variables

Printing variables using a label is an exciting feature of labels. Labels can print the value of variables on a chart by converting them into a string, whereas plotshape has a function for plotting text on a chart but cannot use string series as input for plotshape. The input to the plotshape text parameter should always be a constant. I am giving you an example for your understanding :

In the below code, we are using the label function to print the value of open on the chart.

```
//@version=5
indicator("script09",overlay=true)
if open < high[1]*1.002 and open > high[1]*(1-.002)
    label.new(bar_index,high,xloc=xloc.bar_index,text=str.tostring(open))
```

Check the text=str.tostring(open) parameter inside the label function. The tostring() function takes a value of any float or integer and converts the same into a string. The process of converting a particular type of variable into another type is known as typecasting, and pinescript has functions for converting float and integers into strings using the str.tostring() function and float into integer using the int() function. The open value was converted into a string because the label function can only accept string values, not float ones.

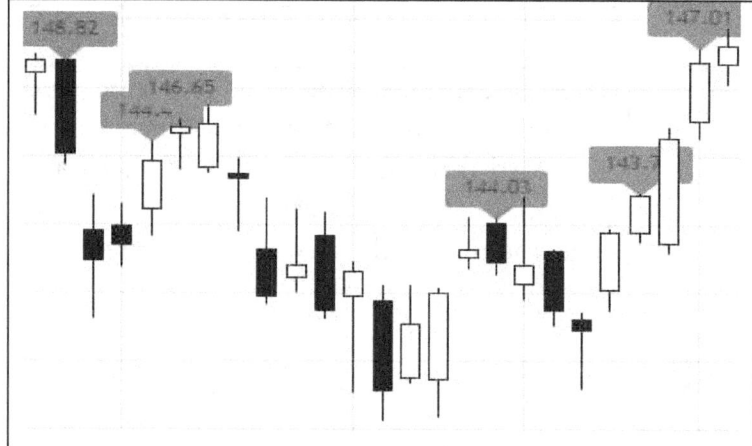

The output of the above script is shown on the left. The open value of the current bar has been printed on the chart

Does the plotshape function have a feature for printing text, and if yes, can the plotshape also print the value of open on the chart as we have done with the label function?

The code of script08 is modified to add the text="O=H" parameter to it

```
01: //@version=5
02: indicator("script10",overlay=true)
03: plotshape(open < high[1]*1.002 and open > high[1]* (1-.002),
```

```
04:    style=shape.xcross,text="O=H",location=location.abovebar,color=color.blue)
```

The out is shown below :

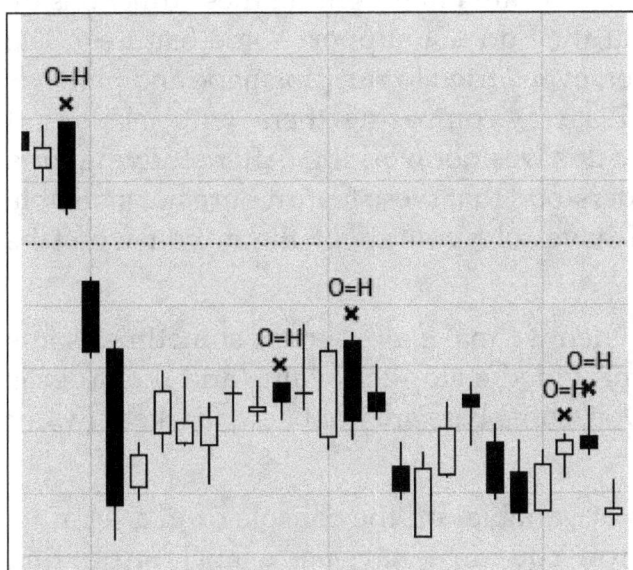

The constant text has been printed above the cross. Can we print the variable values as we did for the label function?

You can try the below code for printing open values on a chart using the plotshape function.

```
01: //@version=5
02: indicator("script10",overlay=true)
03: plotshape(open < high[1]*1.002 and open > high[1]* (1-.002),
04:    style=shape.xcross,text=str.tostring(open),location=location.abovebar,
05 :   color=color.blue)
```

While executing the above script following error was received in the console

```
Processing script...

Compilation error. Line 3: Cannot call 'plotshape' with argument 'text'='call
'str.tostring' (series string)'. An argument of 'series string' type was used but a
'const string' is expected
```

I have the above error message for your interpretation. It cannot call plotshape with text= "series string". You cannot use the plotshape and plotchar functions to plot variable values by converting them into strings.

Label as debugging tool

Why did I discuss all these things in this lesson? Why am I highlighting these functions by giving many examples to support the fact that they do not support some features? The simple answer is that many times as a new coder, even I tried to run plotshape and plotchar inside conditional blocks and was frustrated. I was comparing them with labels and wondered when the label could work and why this was not working. After studying for a while and taking help from some experts, I understood that these features are not available in pinescript for some good reasons. Since I have told you about them, you won't be wasting time understanding them fresh.

Another vital point you should know is that when we make a program, sometimes some things do not go the way we want. If I have provided a stop-loss value and the order is exiting before stop loss, or I wanted to mark Doji, some bars are not being marked. I want to understand my own mistake.

You have no way in pinescript to print values of variables on the console or in a separate file for analyzing them and correcting your error. You can always use a label for printing values of variables on bars for studying them. Let's say I want to know the last high and current open value for my comparison and understanding; then, I can print both using a label function. A quick example is shown below :

```
//@version=5
indicator("script11",overlay=true)
if open < high[1]*1.002 and open > high[1]*(1-.002)
    label.new(bar_index,high,xloc=xloc.bar_index,text=
     str.tostring(high[1])+":"+str.tostring(open))
```

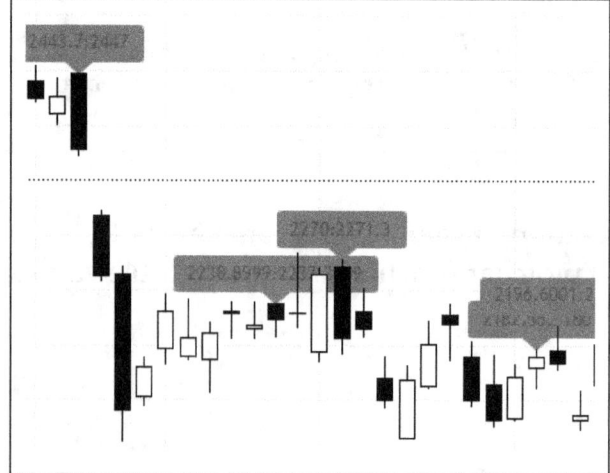

You can use the "+" sign to join two or more strings, as I have done in the above code. See how indentation is done; the last line has 4 space indentations for the "if" block and extra indentation for showing continuation from the last line. The output generated is shown below.

Lesson 8: Loops - Repeating Task

Computers are best known for doing faster work, especially for repeating tasks. Let's say you have to calculate an average for the last 7 periods; then you would have to sum up prices for the last 7 periods and divide them by 7.

Each calculation is termed a task in computer science. Let's assume that the last 7 period prices are 10,9,8,8,9,7,9,10,8 and 7. How will you do the sum? You cannot add all of them at once. You would add 2 of them at a time to arrive at the sum. Overall, you would have to do 6 sums before you arrive at a total sum. If you divide the sum by 7, you will get an average.

Doing the sum six times is a repeating task. This type of repetition can be avoided by using a loop code. In pinescript, we have a "for" loop. The "for" statement allows repeating a block of statements a finite number of times.

In simpler terms, when you write a script and want a particular block of the script to run over and over again a certain number of times, you can use loops instead of writing several script lines.

The "for" Loop

The for loop is used when you know exactly how many times the code is to be executed.

The syntax of the "for" loop is as under:

for *init counter* to *end counter* [*by step*]
　　statement 1 to be repeated
　　statement 1 to be repeated

The "init counter" initializes the initial value for the loop counter. For example, you want to take an average for the last seven close prices; then you can start this counter value from 0 to 6 or 1 to 7 so that seven numbers are exactly covered. If we are using 0 to 6, then 0 is an initialization of the counter, and the end counter value is 6.

Below is the code for calculating a simple moving average for 7 periods on close price.

```
//@version=5
indicator("script13",overlay=true)
sum=0
sum:=sum + close[0]
sum:=sum + close[1]
```

```
sum:=sum + close[2]
sum:=sum + close[3]
sum:=sum + close[4]
sum:=sum + close[5]
sum:=sum + close[6]
closeAverage= sum/7

plot(closeAverage)
```

The same task can be completed by using for loop as under:

```
//@version=5
indicator("script14",overlay=true)
sum = 0.0
for i=0 to 6
    sum :=sum + close[i]
closeAverage= sum/7
plot(closeAverage)
```

The output of the above code is as under :

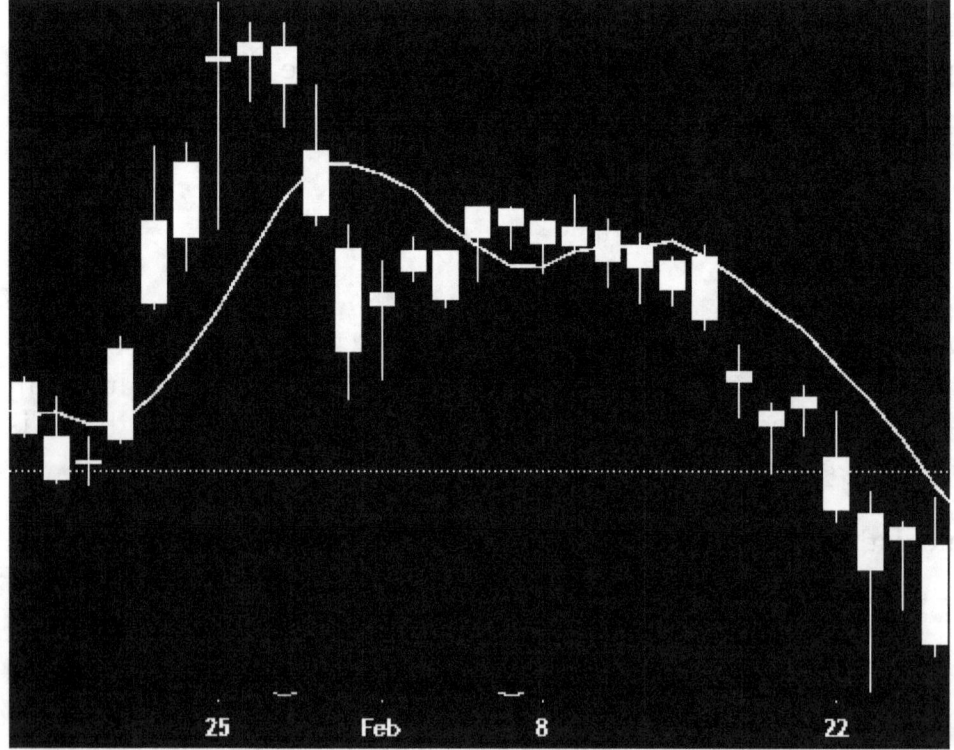

Here in the above code, "i" is a counter variable whose value increases by one unit after the execution of each loop. In the first loop, the value of "i" is "1", and in the second loop, it is 2, and so on.

We already know that the value of historical prices can be accessed by adding [..]. The above code can thus calculate the average close price for the last seven periods.

The "by step" when omitted, as done above, then the default value for an increment is one. After executing each loop, the number after "by step" is the increment number we want to provide to the counter.

For example, say you put for i=0 to 10 by step 2, then the values that counter "i" will take would be 0,2,4,6,8,10.

Similarly, if you want reverse counting, you can do i=10 to 0 by step -1, and the values for "i" would be 10,9,8,7,6,5,4,3,2,1 and 0.

The break Statement

Each statement execution consumes time and resources of the system; further, in some cases, you may want to stop the loop in between before it reaches the counter's end value. In such cases, you can use a "break" statement to interrupt the loop and execute the remaining statements.

Below is an example wherein I want to count the last engulf bar location from the current bar position.

```
//@version=5
//code to place counting of last engulf from the current bar
indicator("script15",overlay=true,max_bars_back=200)
lastEngulf = 0
for i=1 to 100
    if high[i-1] > high[i] and low[i-1] < low[i]
        lastEngulf := i-1
        break
myLabel = label.new(x=bar_index,y=high,text=str.tostring(lastEngulf))
plotshape(high > high[1] and low < low[1])
label.delete(myLabel[1])
```

In the above code, I have used some new instructions for demonstration. The above will start bar counting from the current bar in a backward direction. Once the engulfing bar is found, the counter's value is stored in the variable "lastEngulf", and the "for" loop is exited by the "break" instruction. The "break" statement allows skipping the remaining loop and statements after the loops are executed.

Here, the label.new is executed with the statement "myLabel =". The label.new creates a new variable, and the information of this label is stored in the "myLabel" variable, whose type is a label. The label drawing command is since executed on the formation of each bar; we need to delete the last label to have only one label on the screen.

As shown above, any label can be deleted by a "label.delete" command.

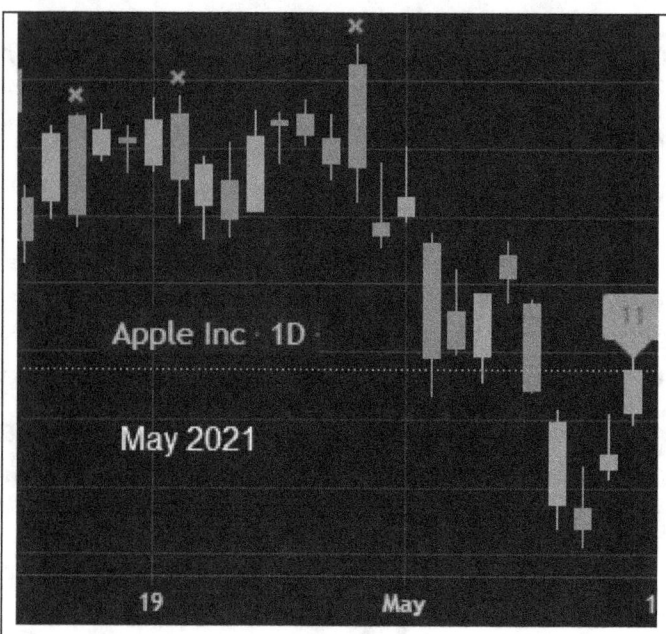

On the left side is the output generated by the script. Each engulf bar has been marked with a plotshape function.

From the last bar, the location of the nearest engulf bar is 11 bars.

The while loop statement

Similar to the "for loop" statement, while loop is also used for repeating certain statements. A "while" loop allows the execution of a set of statements till the condition provided in the while loop is true. The loop stops once the condition becomes false. The "while" loop has been introduced in version 5 of the pine script and is not available in previous versions.

If the "for" loop was already available in pinescript, why did the developers introduce the "while" loop? How is a "while" loop different from a "for" loop? What are the situations where a "while" loop is more suitable than a "for" loop? We try to figure out answers to all our queries. Before that, take an example:

```
01: //@version=5
02: indicator("While Loop",overlay=true)
03: i=0
04: sum=0.0
05: while(i<7)
06:     sum:=sum+close[i]
07:     i:=i+1
08: myAvg7 = sum/7
09: plot(myAvg7)
```

The above script for calculating simple moving averages uses a while loop. Try to identify differences with for loop.

The general syntax for the execution of a "while" loop is as under:

```
While (condition)
    Statement 1 to be repeated
    Statement 2 to be repeated
    ...........
    Statement 3 to be repeated
```

In the above code, "i" acts as a counter. Before the loop, "i" is set to zero, and in the subsequent loops, the value of "i" is increased. The "while" condition is set such that if the value of "i" is increased, the condition is satisfied. The rest of the code is similar to for loop code.

The major difference from the loop is:

1. A counter can be changed from within a block of statements, which is not allowed in for loop
2. Unlike the "for" loop, a user has to manage counters in the "while" loop. In the "for" loop, the loop changes the counter automatically, and a user is not required to use a statement like i:=i+1 to manage the counter.

Why "while" loop was required?

1. All programming languages have for and while loop
2. In the "for" loop, you already know the number of times you want to run a repetition of a particular set of statements, While if you don't know the exact number of times the statement will be executed, you keep an option to change the condition from within the statement block. This is an additional feature provided by the "while" loop.

Lesson 9: Setting up Alert

PineScript allows you to set an alert on real-time prices, so you never miss any opportunity. The alerts can be set in the script for any custom conditions you may like. In this lesson, setting alerts through pinescript is discussed. Once the alert condition is satisfied, a user gets a pop-up window, sound notification, or an SMS or email, depending on the configuration.

Setting Alert from TradingView Interface

Pine script's alert-creating window can be opened by pressing alt+A. You can also open the window by clicking the alert icon provided in the right icon column of the tradingview platform.

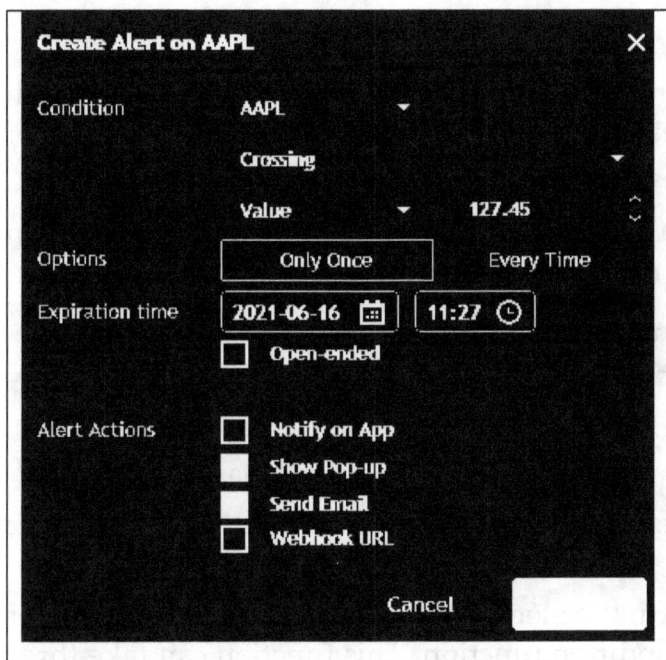

The alert setting window has a simple drop menu for selecting options from the list of alternatives.

If I am on the Apple Inc chart, Alt+A will provide the option to set an alert on the apple inc scrip only. If you are opening it for the first time, you won't have many options under conditions except the scrip AAPL.

The next drop-down is for selecting conditions for which an alert must be triggered.

All the options available in this drop-down are related to price, whether it's moving up by a certain per cent or is in a predefined channel of fixed upper and lower bound. If you want to set an alert on abnormally high volume activity, you probably won't be able to set it from this user window because you don't have the option to do so.

Further options that can be set in are expiration time and frequency. I usually set it only once, and an expiration time can be as per your requirement. After the expiry of an alert, the tradingview server stops tracking alert requests. The expiry is provided to reduce the burden on the server.

Alerts can be served via email or popup messages with sound. Intraday traders keep the tradingview window open for the entire day, a pop-up message is best for intraday traders. If you are a long-term investor, ask for an alert via email. Once the alert is created, there is no need to keep your tradingview account login for tracking. If you require pop-up messages, you must keep your account open. The tradingview server keeps track of all alert requests 24X7. Once the condition of the alert is fulfilled, the alert is triggered and sent to you. For premium customers, i.e. paid customers, unlimited SMS service is also available.

Setting Custom Alert

In the last section, we observed that there are limited conditions for setting alerts through the alert creation window. If you want to set an alert on high-volume activity, you cannot set an alert as the option for setting such an alert is not available.

Through pinescript, we can create an option in the alert creation window. After the option is created in the alert creation window, you can set an alert.

Below is the example for creating an alert on locating engulfing bar.

```
//@version=5
indicator("script15",overlay=true)
alertcondition(high > high[1] and low < low[1],"Engulfing","Engulfing Bar")
plot(ta.sma(close,7))
```

The third line of the script creates an option in the alert creation window. The function for setting the custom alert option is the alertcondition function. This function can take three inputs from the user. The syntax of alertcondition is as under:

```
alertcondition(condition,[title],[message])
```

The first and compulsory input to alertcondition is condition. When the condition is "true", an alert can be triggered. The second input is the alert name, and the third is the message you want to receive while receiving an alert.

On line no. 3 in script15, the condition is for engulfing, the name of the alert is "Engulfing", and the message on the condition being "true" is "Engulfing Bar". The last line is plot(ta.sma(close,7)); this is to plot a simple moving average for 7 periods.

Note that the above code does not create an alert or trigger an alert when the condition provided becomes true. The above code only provides an option in the alert creation window to set an alert.

The code alertcondition() is not creating output and only creating an option in the alert creation window. But the script needs at least one output function like plot, drawshape, etc. otherwise, the script generates an error that 'script must have at least one output function call'. Therefore, we have included one plot function to plot a simple moving average for 7 periods.

The above is the alert creation window that can be accessed by pressing Alt+A. If you have added your script to the chart, you can select the script's name, and all alert titles of alterconditions() appear in the selection drop-down menu. Rest is easy to configure. Once the alert is set, the server stores a copy of the script code and an alert request on the TradingView server for 24X7 tracking. Even if the script is removed from the chart or the code is changed or deleted, the alert keeps running on the server till the expiration time is reached.

Engulf Screener through PineScript

Setting alerts for individual stock can be time-consuming. There may be a need to generate a quick screener for gap up, open = high, open = low, engulfing pattern, etc. For such a quick screener, we have a small script presented below for use.

The limitation of this script is that it can scan about 40 scrips at a time. If you need to screen more than 40 stock, create another script. You are required to add this script to the chart for screening.

Below is the script for screening engulfing pattern.

```
//@version=5
indicator("Engulf Screener", overlay = true)

condition() => high > high[1] and low < low[1]

AAPL_result = request.security('AAPL','D',condition())
MSFT_result = request.security('MSFT','D',condition())
AMZN_result = request.security('AMZN','D',condition())
GOOG_result = request.security('GOOG','D',condition())
GOOGL_result = request.security('GOOGL','D',condition())
FB_result = request.security('FB','D',condition())
TSLA_result = request.security('TSLA','D',condition())
NVDA_result = request.security('NVDA','D',condition())
PYPL_result = request.security('PYPL','D',condition())
ASML_result = request.security('ASML','D',condition())
CMCSA_result = request.security('CMCSA','D',condition())
ADBE_result = request.security('ADBE','D',condition())
INTC_result = request.security('INTC','D',condition())
CSCO_result = request.security('CSCO','D',condition())
NFLX_result = request.security('NFLX','D',condition())
PEP_result = request.security('PEP','D',condition())
AVGO_result = request.security('AVGO','D',condition())
TMUS_result = request.security('TMUS','D',condition())
COST_result = request.security('COST','D',condition())
TXN_result = request.security('TXN','D',condition())
PDD_result = request.security('PDD','D',condition())
QCOM_result = request.security('QCOM','D',condition())
CHTR_result = request.security('CHTR','D',condition())
AMGN_result = request.security('AMGN','D',condition())
SBUX_result = request.security('SBUX','D',condition())
```

```
AMAT_result = request.security('AMAT','D',condition())
INTU_result = request.security('INTU','D',condition())
JD_result = request.security('JD','D',condition())
ISRG_result = request.security('ISRG','D',condition())
BKNG_result = request.security('BKNG','D',condition())
ZM_result = request.security('ZM','D',condition())
AMD_result = request.security('AMD','D',condition())
MU_result = request.security('MU','D',condition())
MDLZ_result = request.security('MDLZ','D',condition())
LRCX_result = request.security('LRCX','D',condition())
GILD_result = request.security('GILD','D',condition())
ADP_result = request.security('ADP','D',condition())
CSX_result = request.security('CSX','D',condition())
FISV_result = request.security('FISV','D',condition())

label1 = '------Engulf Screener -------\n'  // \n is equivalent to return button on your keyboard

label1:=AAPL_result ? label1+'AAPL\n' : label1
label1:=MSFT_result ? label1+'MSFT\n' : label1
label1:=AMZN_result ? label1+'AMZN\n' : label1
label1:=GOOG_result ? label1+'GOOG\n' : label1
label1:=GOOGL_result ? label1+'GOOGL\n' : label1
label1:=FB_result ? label1+'FB\n' : label1
label1:=TSLA_result ? label1+'TSLA\n' : label1
label1:=NVDA_result ? label1+'NVDA\n' : label1
label1:=PYPL_result ? label1+'PYPL\n' : label1
label1:=ASML_result ? label1+'ASML\n' : label1
label1:=CMCSA_result ? label1+'CMCSA\n' : label1
label1:=ADBE_result ? label1+'ADBE\n' : label1
label1:=INTC_result ? label1+'INTC\n' : label1
label1:=CSCO_result ? label1+'CSCO\n' : label1
label1:=NFLX_result ? label1+'NFLX\n' : label1
label1:=PEP_result ? label1+'PEP\n' : label1
label1:=AVGO_result ? label1+'AVGO\n' : label1
label1:=TMUS_result ? label1+'TMUS\n' : label1
label1:=COST_result ? label1+'COST\n' : label1
label1:=TXN_result ? label1+'TXN\n' : label1
label1:=PDD_result ? label1+'PDD\n' : label1
label1:=QCOM_result ? label1+'QCOM\n' : label1
```

```
label1:=CHTR_result ? label1+'CHTR\n' : label1
label1:=AMGN_result ? label1+'AMGN\n' : label1
label1:=SBUX_result ? label1+'SBUX\n' : label1
label1:=AMAT_result ? label1+'AMAT\n' : label1
label1:=INTU_result ? label1+'INTU\n' : label1
label1:=JD_result ? label1+'JD\n' : label1
label1:=ISRG_result ? label1+'ISRG\n' : label1
label1:=BKNG_result ? label1+'BKNG\n' : label1
label1:=ZM_result ? label1+'ZM\n' : label1
label1:=AMD_result ? label1+'AMD\n' : label1
label1:=MU_result ? label1+'MU\n' : label1
label1:=MDLZ_result ? label1+'MDLZ\n' : label1
label1:=LRCX_result ? label1+'LRCX\n' : label1
label1:=GILD_result ? label1+'GILD\n' : label1
label1:=ADP_result ? label1+'ADP\n' : label1
label1:=CSX_result ? label1+'CSX\n' : label1
label1:=FISV_result ? label1+'FISV\n' : label1

caption = label.new(bar_index, close, label1,color=color.blue,
  textcolor=color.black,style=label.style_labeldown,
  yloc = yloc.price)
label.delete(caption[1])
```

You can notice that this script is very long due to the repetitive nature of the code.

The result produced from this script is shown below :

You can add this script to any chart, and the result is the same. No name of scrip appears after execution of this script, which means that on 14 May 2021, for about 40 equities for which it was run, no engulfing pattern could be found.

I can quickly change the second line of the script, providing the condition to scan open = high of the last bar.

```
condition() => open < high[1]*(1 +0.002) and open > high[1]*(1-0.002)
```

And after making logical changes to the title and label caption result is as under :

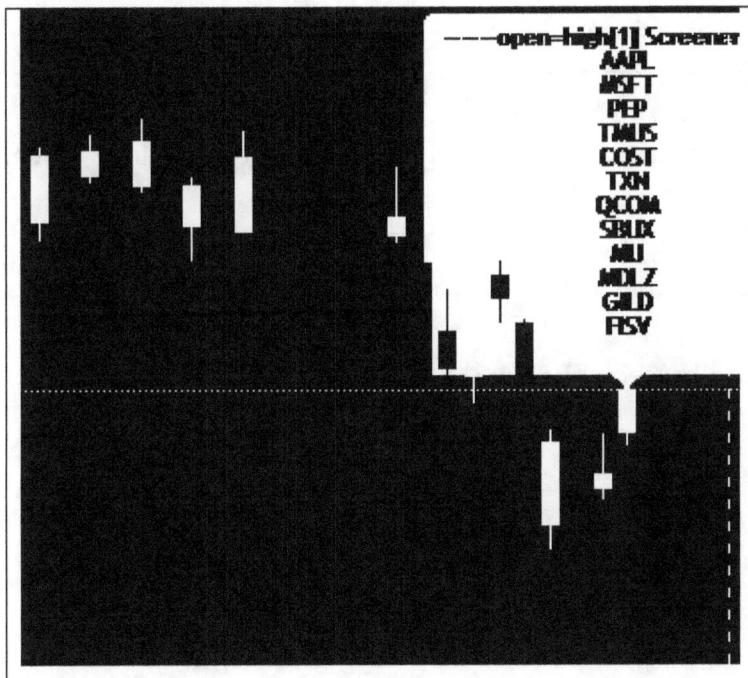

On 14 May, I could find 12 equities that have open = high[1]. Names of all scrips are shown on the label of the last bar.

Explanation of Screener Code

The first line is a declaration of indicator function wherein the script's name is "Engulf Screener", and the overlay has been set to "true", i.e. the label or draw is on the chart and not below the chart.

```
//@version=5
indicator("Engulf Screener", overlay = true)
condition() => high > high[1] and low < low[1]

AAPL_result = request.security('AAPL','D',condition())
```

The second line is a function that is true when the condition is true and false when the condition is false. More on functions are covered in the next lesson. Here, in the condition function, we have provided a condition for engulfing pattern, i.e. when the current bar's high is higher than the previous bar's high and the close is lower than the previous bar's low.

In the third line, a new function has been used, i.e. security. The security function can fetch scrip data other than the scrip displayed on the chart. You can also fetch data or results of any timeframe.

A simple syntax of the security function is provided below:

```
request.security(symbol, resolution, expression)
```

Say you are on APPLE INC daily chart and want to access apple inc weekly close price; you can use :

```
aapl_close = request.security('AAPL', "W", close)
```

The resolution, i.e. timeframe supported by security are :

1S, 5S, 15S, 30S - for seconds intervals
from 1 to 1440 for minutes
from 1D to 365D for days
from 1W to 52W for weeks
from 1M to 12M for months

Here in the above example, we have sought "close" value. The security function provides AAPL's weekly "close" value. You can also directly seek calculated values like:

```
aapl_return_weekly = request.security('AAPL,"W",(close[1]-close)/close)
```

However, note that the security function can be used only 40 times in a script. The limit is placed to avoid an unnecessary burden on server resources that all users share.

The label1 is declared by using the "=" sign. The label1 is a string, and it stores the value of '------Engulf Screener --------\n'. Please note that "\n" means the return key of your keyboard. This instructs the system for a line change.

```
label1 = '------Engulf Screener --------\n'
```

As and when engulf condition becomes true, the scrip name is added to the string label1 by use of a "+" sign

```
label1:=AAPL_result ? label1+'AAPL\n' : label1
```

Here for conditional assignment "?" operator has been used in place of the "iff" condition. The above can also be re-written as

```
label1:=iff(AAPL_result,label1+'AAPL\n',label1)
```

```
caption = label.new(bar_index, close, label1,color=color.blue,
  textcolor=color.black,style=label.style_labeldown,
  yloc = yloc.price)
```

The above is a single instruction spread over three lines. Indentation of two spaces has been provided to instruct the system that the instruction is continuing on the line. We already know how a label is created. Here, we have added "caption =" before the label.new command. This provides the "caption" as the name of the label.

```
label.delete(caption[1])
```

This last line instructs the system to delete the previously created label. Note that there is a maximum limit for creating labels on the chart. To remain within that limit and to avoid labelling over every bar, it is suggested that previous labels are deleted before a new label is created.

Lesson 10: Functions

The main speciality of computers is to automate repetition work. In coding, sometimes you may be required to repeat codes again and again. Repetition, to some extent, can be avoided by using functions. You may have seen in previous examples that we use a simple moving average function to calculate the average. We just provided close and some periods; the average is calculated and stored in the variable on the left side of the "=" mark.

Functions are like a black box, you give input, and you get an output. You do not know how the actual calculation is done. For example, if you want to calculate the rsi of close for the last 7 periods, you can use :

```
myRSI = rsi(close,7)
```

You may not know the formula of rsi, yet with the help of a built-in function, you can calculate rsi very easily and quickly.

In simpler terms, functions take input through the two brackets that appear after their name and provide output that can be saved in the left side variable of the "=" mark. Till now, we have encountered many functions, a few of which are enumerated below:

```
indicator()
plot()
plotshape()
drawchar()
label.new()
ta.sma()
alertcondition()
request.security()
label.delete()
str.tostring()
```

All functions have a name followed by bracket "()"; the input to the function is provided in these brackets and is separated by commas. These functions make code more readable and allow coders to code faster. The pinescript has many built-in functions to allow coders to focus on their indicators and strategy; using built-in functions reduces the coding complexity.

Common functions that have not yet been studied and are used frequently in pinescript are as under :

ta.atr(length)	ta.crossover(x, y)
ta.barssince(condition)	ta.crossunder(x, y)

ta.ema(source,length) ta.correlation(source_a, source_b, length) ta.sar(start, inc, max) ta.valuewhen(condition, source, occurrence) ta.stoch(source, high, low, length) [middle, upper, lower] = ta.bb(series, length, mult) ta.cmo(series, length) ta.cog(source, length)	ta.dmi(diLength, adxSmoothing) [middle, upper, lower] = ta.kc(series, length, mult) ta.mfi(series, length) ta.pivothigh(source, leftbars, rightbars) ta.pivotlow(source, leftbars, rightbars) [superTrend, dir] = ta.supertrend(factor, atrPeriod) ta.wpr(length)

Some of the above are technical indicators; we would study some of them, beginning with in-built technical indicators.

Built-in Technical Indicators

We have already studied simple moving average(sma) and relative strength index (rsi); now, have a quick look at other built-in indicators offered by pinescript.

Average True Value

The average true value is a measure of market volatility. Typically 14 periods are selected as input for its calculation. The result of average true value or ATR is in terms of absolute prices. If the price is 50 and volatility is 10%, ATR gives a value of 5. ATR value is most frequently used for setting stop-losses. The syntax of average true value (atr) is as under :

```
atr_value=ta.atr(length)
```

The value of atr is always positive. Here is an example code and the resultant output.

```
//@version=5
indicator("script16",overlay=false)
myAtr = ta.atr(14)
plot(myAtr)
```

Here in the above code, the overlay has been set to "false", meaning we want the output to be printed below the chart.

Below is the output of atr code. The highest value of ATR was about USD 4 around the end of the first week of March. Here, we can also observe that the prices have turned around the same point. This atr value can be used to set a realistic target or stop loss depending on the volatility of a market.

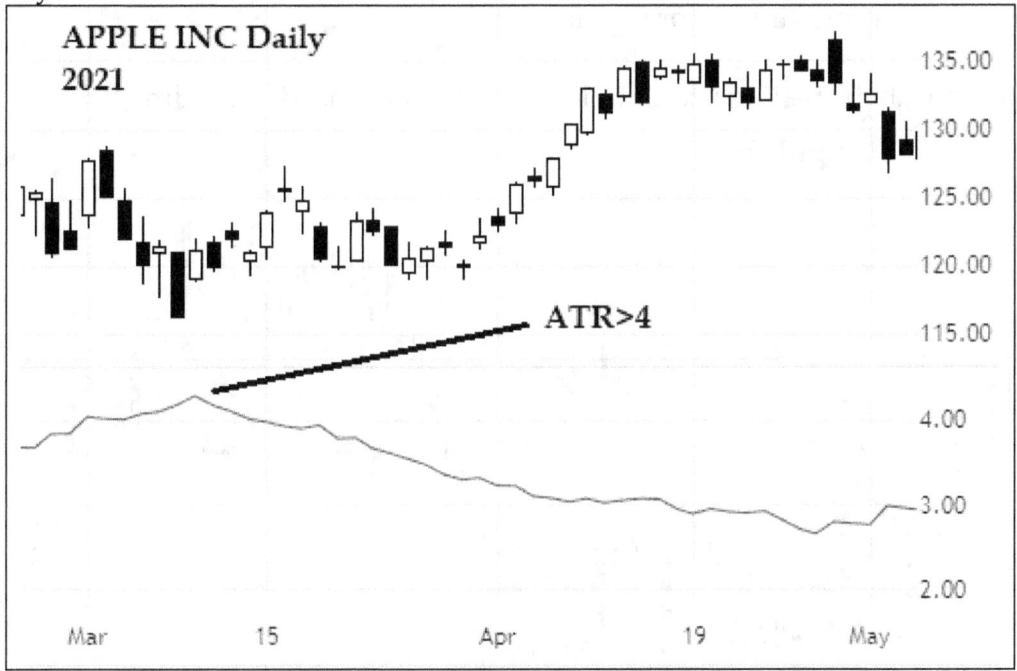

Exponential Moving Average

Exponential moving average(ema) is another moving average wherein more weightage is given to the recent values, and less weightage is given to older values. Exponential moving averages are an improvement over simple moving averages. However, due to the complexity of the calculation, traders and investors still prefer to use a simple moving average. Now, since we have a built-in function for ema, we can implement it similar to sma. It will help if you replace sma with ema.

The syntax for ema is as under :
```
myEMA = ta.ema(source,length)
```

You may implement it yourself. I am not providing a code for it. Assume it as your assignment work. In the above syntax, my EMA is the result variable, and the source could be open, close, high, low, or volume values for which you want to calculate ema. The length is the period for which ema has to be calculated.

Parabolic SAR

Parabolic SAR (parabolic stop and reverse) is an indicator developed by J. Welles Wilder, Jr. The parabolic SAR helps traders and investors find potential reversals in the trend of prices of equity, commodity, or forex prices.

A chart with parabolic SAR is presented below for better understanding.

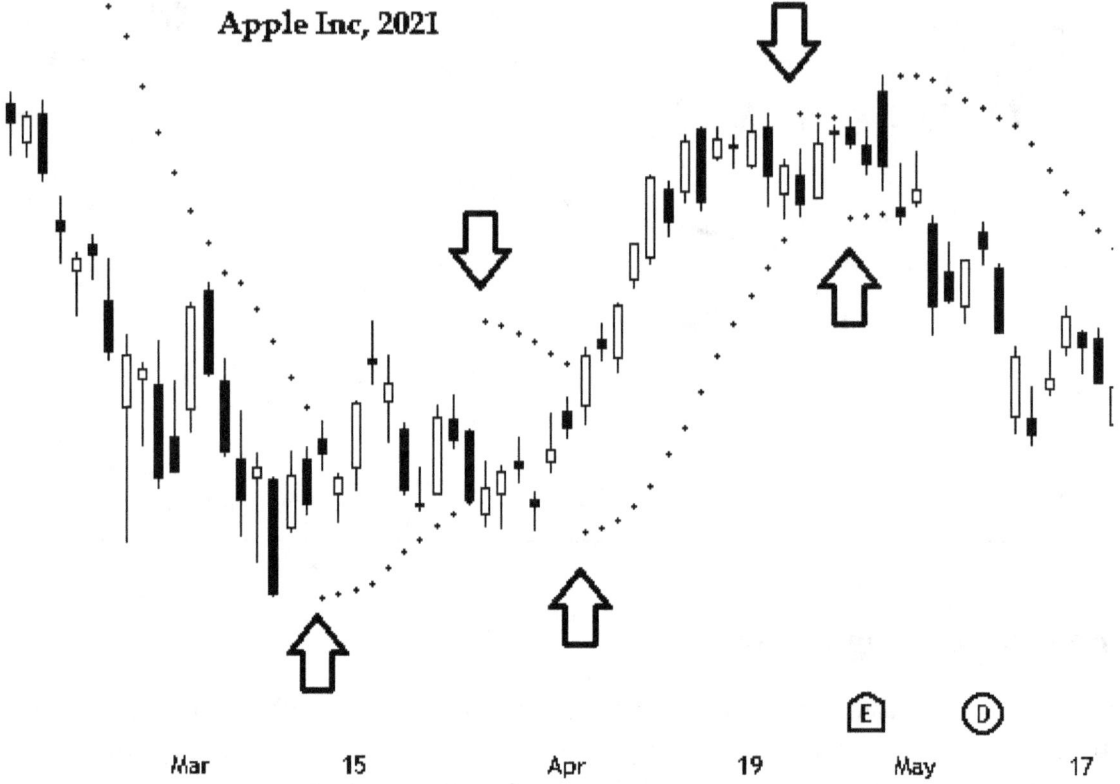

The strategy to trade with a parabolic SAR is to go long when dots are below the price and go short when dots are above the price. These dots can also be used as a trailing stop when you have already taken a trade. You may require an additional filter or indicator to confirm trend change before actual trade can be taken.

A typical syntax of parabolic sar is as under :

```
mySAR = ta.sar(start, acceleration factor, max)
```

Typical settings are start= 0.02, acceleration factor = 0.02, and max = 0.20. The more is acceleration, the more closely SAR places stop-losses. The more the acceleration value, indicates more reversals. Hit and trial is the best method to select a value of acceleration depending on volatility, time frame, and your requirement.

The code to implement Parabolic SAR is given below.

```
//@version=5
indicator("script17",overlay=true)
start = 0.02
inc = 0.02
max = 0.2
mySAR = ta.sar(start, inc, max)
plot(mySAR,style=plot.style_circles)
```

Correlation

In statistics, correlation is the degree (calculated between 1 and -1) to which two variables move with respect to another variable. Say we have two equities from a sector, and the price of one equity rises; would the price of the other equity also rise?

Correlation between two price series is calculated; if the correction value is 0, that means these two series are not related to each other. If the correlation value is 1, it means that the prices of two equities are perfectly related and move in tandem with one another. If the correlation value is above 80, traders and investors take those two equities for pair trading.

An equity's correlation with a broader index can also be calculated for trading purposes. The syntax of correlation is as under:

```
corel_value=ta.correlation(Source1, Source2, length)
```

Plotted below is an example of the correlation between NDX (Nasdaq 100 index) and Apple Inc.

The value of correlation is below 90 before Apr 2021. That means that Apple and Index were not closely linked before April 2021.

From April 2021, you can consider Apple and Nasdaq as a pair for pair trading purposes by selling one and buying another for profitable trade with minimum risk.

The source code in the pine script for the above correlation chart is given below for your ready reference.

```
//@version=5
indicator("script18",overlay=false)
sourceA = close
sourceB = request.security("NDX","",close)
corel_value = ta.correlation(sourceA,sourceB,40)
plot(corel_value)
```

We have used the request.security function for importing closing values of "NDX" in this chart. You can note that I have left the timeframe/ resolution blank under the security function. This is done so that the close's resolution imported from NDX has the current resolution of the chart.

The Chande Momentum Oscillator

Tushar Chande developed the Chande Momentum Oscillator (CMO). The indicator value ranges between -100 and 100. A value of more than 50 is considered overbought, and a value below -50 is considered oversold. The syntax of the chande momentum oscillator is as under

```
cmo_value = ta.cmo(series, length)
```

The CMO is more reactive than RSI and, therefore, more preferred over RSI. Many traders and investors calculate a 10-period moving average of CMO, which is then used as a signal line. The CMO value when crosses above this signal line of 10 periods moving average, the market is considered bullish, and the market is considered bearish if the CMO value is below the signal line.

The source code for implementation of CMO is given below for ready reference

```
//@version=5
indicator("script19",overlay=false)
cmo_value=ta.cmo(close,14)
cmo_avg = ta.ema(cmo_value,7)
plot(cmo_avg,color=color.red)
plot(cmo_value,color=color.blue)
```

Needless to say that a single indicator cannot be used for taking a trade, the use of other indicators or candlestick patterns is advisable.

Center of Gravity

The Center of Gravity (COG) is another oscillator-type indicator. It is a recent oscillator indicator created by a weighted moving average. The main benefit is that it has less lag than moving average indicators. The COG is also used to locate points of resistance and supports on the chart. The COG also helps in the identification of clear turning points. The syntax of the COG indicator is as under :

```
cog_value = ta.cog(source, length)
```

The buy position is created when the cog is at the bottom, and a sell is initiated when the cog is turning down from the top. The cog can also be used for finding the divergence between cog and price to take action. Some traders also prefer to create a signal line, i.e. a simple moving average of COG and take trade upon their crossover.

The source script for the COG is provided below for ready reference:

```
//@version=5
indicator("script20",overlay=false)
cog_value=ta.cog(close,10)
cog_avg = ta.sma(cog_value,7)
plot(cog_value,color=color.blue)
plot(cog_avg,color=color.red)
```

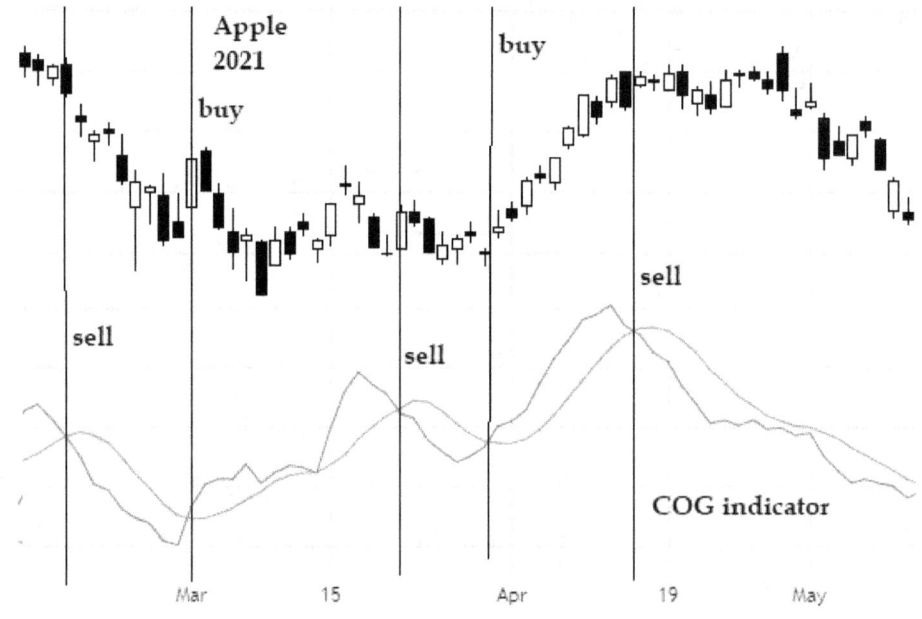

As you can observe from the Apple Inc Daily Chart, the buy/sell signals generated by this system are reasonably accurate. However, an additional indicator or candlestick pattern is advisable for trading.

Money Flow Index

The money flow index is another oscillator-type indicator that uses price and volume to provide oversold and overbought signals. Only two inputs are required for this: source, i.e. open, close, high, low, ohlc4, hlc3, or hl2, and the number of bars you want to include in the calculation. The ohlc4 means an average price of open, high, low, and close; hlc3 means an average of high, low, and close, whereas hl2 is the bar's midpoint. However, hlc3 is recommended for the calculation of MFI.

```
mfi_value = ta.mfi(series, length)
```

The money flow index ranges from 0 to 100. A value above 80 is considered overbought, and a value below 20 is considered oversold. The divergence between the price and the MFI is also considered for identifying a potential reversal point. The money flow is calculated by multiplying the typical price (hlc3) with volume to arrive at MFI.

As discussed earlier, some traders also prefer to use signal line along with MFI. The signal is created by calculating the average of MFI. A typical implementation of MFI is provided below.

```
//@version=5
indicator("script21",overlay=false)
mfi_value=ta.mfi(hlc3,14)
mfi_avg = ta.sma(mfi_value,7)
plot(mfi_value,color=color.blue)
plot(mfi_avg,color=color.red)
```

The chart of the MFI indicator on APPLE INC daily is provided below for ready reference:

The signals generated by MFI on APPLE INC, Daily is above, and you can see more noise than the COG index we used on the same chart. However, the MFI can capture trend changes somewhat earlier than COG. Additional filters are needed to have more clear trading signals.

Stoch

It calculates Stochastic and is a momentum indicator with a value between 0 and 100. Again the sensitivity can be adjusted by the period's length over which it is calculated. You can find overbought and oversold from this indicator, which can also be used to locate the divergence between price and stochastic. The syntax of stoch is as under :

```
Stoch_value = ta.stoch(source, high, low, length)
```

Many traders create moving averages of stochastic to use them as signal lines. An implementation of stochastic with a signal line is shown below.

```
//@version=5
indicator("script22",overlay=false)
stoch_value=ta.stoch(close,high,low,14)
stoch_avg = ta.sma(stoch_value,7)
plot(stoch_value,color=color.blue)
plot(stoch_avg,color=color.red)
```

The resultant chart is as under :

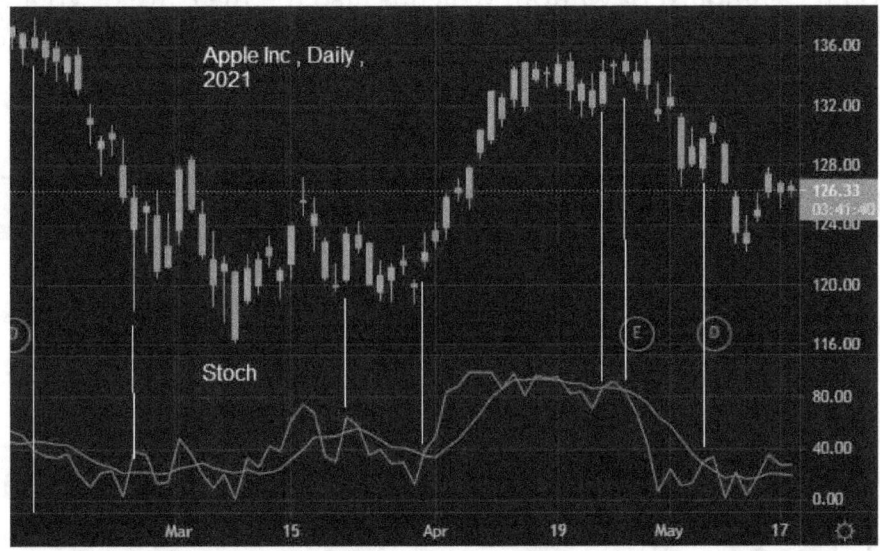

The above chart has much noise due to the high volatility in the stoch. This problem can be solved by taking 3-period sma of stoch value and taking sma of 6 or 7 periods for signal. The resultant chart is as under :

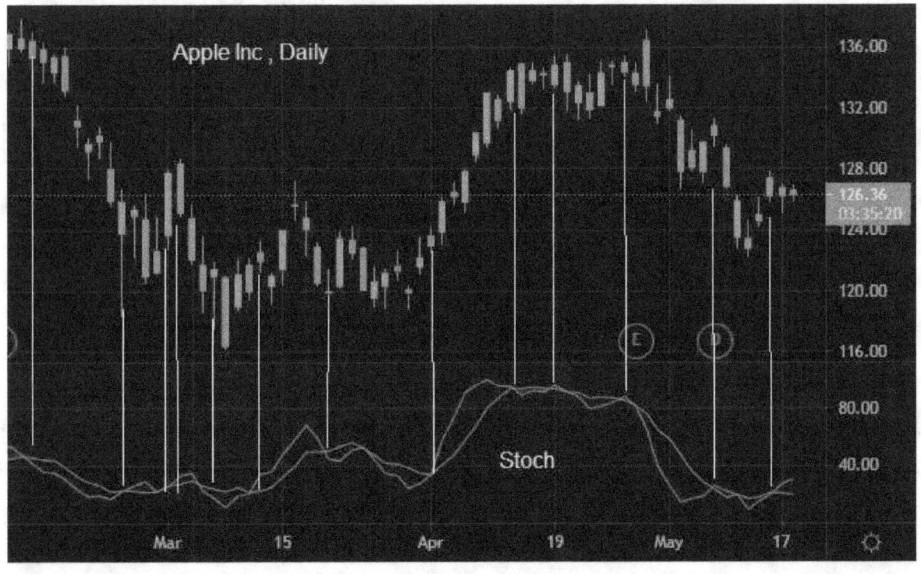

Bollinger Bands

Bollinger Band assumes that prices are distributed around the mean with normal distribution. For any normal distribution, 95% of values always remain within +/- twice of standard deviation.

Therefore, one can always be sure with a 95% probability that the prices lie inside the Bollinger band. If the price crosses Bollinger Band, one can always take a position. The band is based on the standard deviation, which is also the measure of volatility. The band considers volatility, and the band's size keeps changing with the change in standard deviation.

The syntax of Bollinger band is as under:

> [middle, upper, lower] = ta.bb(series, length, standard deviation)

The default value for the series is close, the length is 20, and the standard deviation is 2. A chart showing Bollinger Band on Apple Inc is shown below:

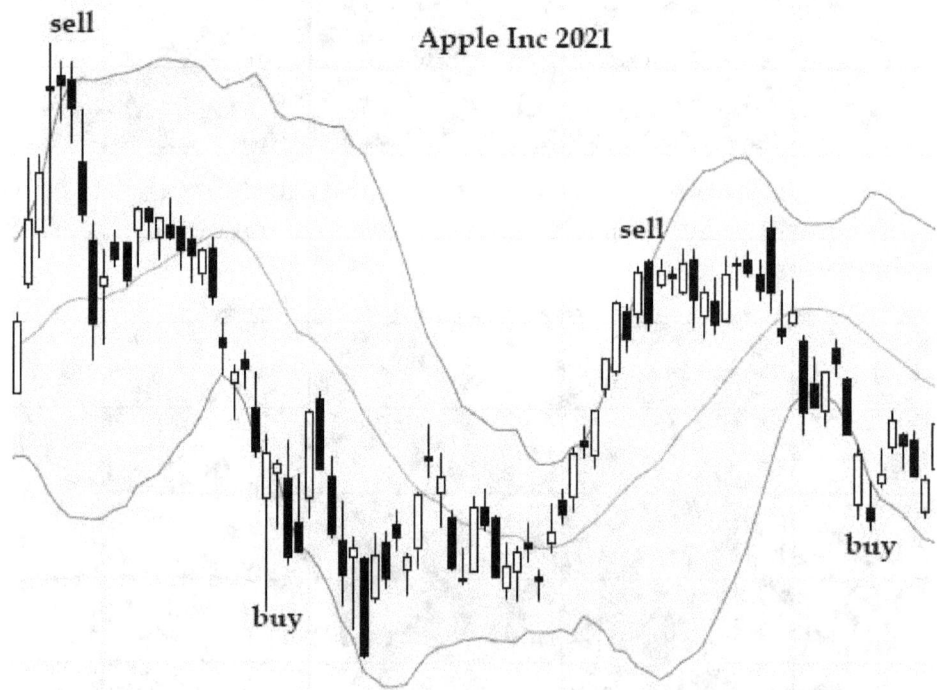

In the above chart, sell and buy positions have been marked. A sell position is possible once the prices rise above the upper band and candlestick confirmation is obtained. A buy position is possible once the price dip is below the lower band and a candlestick pattern is found.

The source code for Bollinger band is given below:

```
//@version=5
indicator("script23",overlay=true)
[mean,upperBand, lowerBand] = ta.bb(close,20,2)
plot(upperBand,color=color.blue)
plot(lowerBand,color=color.blue)
plot(mean,color=color.green)
```

Williams %R

Williams %R is a momentum indicator that uses price to provide oversold and overbought signals. The range of the indicator is 0 to -100, wherein -20 is overbought, and -80 is oversold. The current price is compared with high and low values in the last lookback period.

Syntax of Williams %R is as under:

```
wpr_value = ta.wpr(length)
```

I am not providing a script for its implementation; consider this an assignment. Below is the chart developed by Williams %R. The WPR is implemented similarly to the "stoch" of the previous section. Make a signal line by taking a long period average.

On the left, WPR is implemented using a signal line. The line for overbought and oversold can also be differently coloured for better visualization

Keltner Channels

Keltner Channels are similar to Bollinger bands. Keltner channels are also based on volatility; however, unlike standard deviance in the case of the Bollinger band, here they are ATR values. The upper and lower bands are typically defined as twice ATR values.

Syntax of Keltner Channels is as under:

```
[middle, upper, lower] = ta.kc(series, length, multi)
```

The typical values for kc inputs are series = close, length=20 and multiplier = 2. The middle mean line is 20 periods EMA, whereas the upper and lower bands are twice ATR.

The trending strategy on the Keltner channel could be similar to that of the Bollinger band. The slope of the channel can also indicate trend strength. Below is a chart with Keltner Channels.

The source code for the Keltner channel is provided below for quick reference:

```
//@version=5
indicator("script24",overlay=true)
[mean,upperBand, lowerBand] = ta.kc(close,20,2)
plot(upperBand,color=color.blue)
plot(lowerBand,color=color.blue)
plot(mean,color=color.green)
```

Directional Movement Index

The directional movement index is used to find a trend in prices. It does this by comparing the present price with the highest and lowest prices compared with the past period. The syntax of dmi is as under :

[diplus, diminus, adx] =ta.dmi(diLength, adxSmoothing)

The dmi function provides three outputs, one is DI+, another is DI-, and an average of both is ADX. The default input for both diLength and adxSmoothing is 14. When the DI- is above DI+, there is downward pressure; when DI+ is above DI-, there is upward pressure, and one can expect prices to rise. Whereas ADX, the average of both DI+ and DI-, does not show direction but is an indicator of momentum. The crossover of DI+ and DI- are normally used as trade signals. When DI+ crosses over DI-, long trade is taken, and when DI- crosses above DI+ short position is taken.

Below is the chart showing DMI in action:

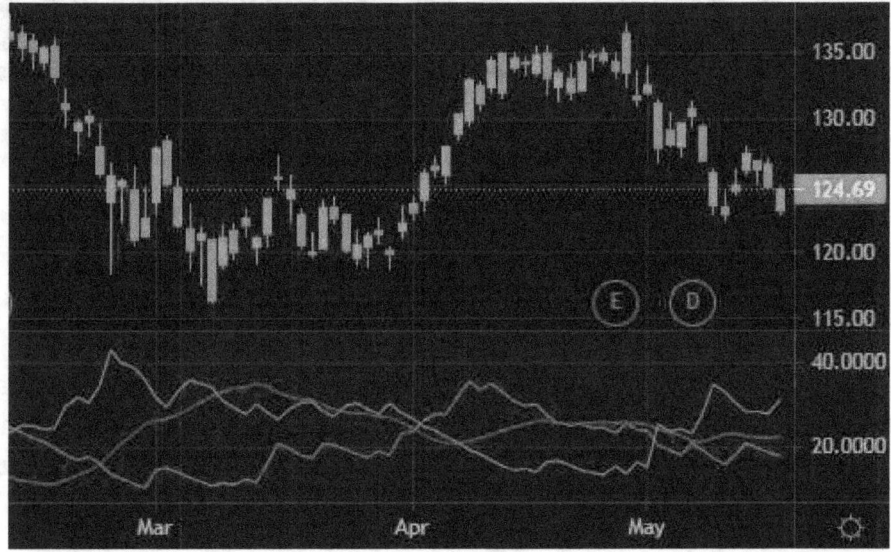

SuperTrend

Supertrend is a trend following indicators like moving averages. Supertrend is created using ATR values multiplied by a multiplier. Supertrend is a lagging indicator; your entry or exit based on a supertrend may be late. You can use RSI, SAR, MACD, or any other technical indicator with a supertrend for refining signals.

[superTrend, dir] = ta.supertrend(multi, atrPeriod)

The default parameters for supertrend are 3 and 10; when you decrease these parameters, buy and sell signals increase, and noise also increases. A neat implementation of supertrend is provided below:

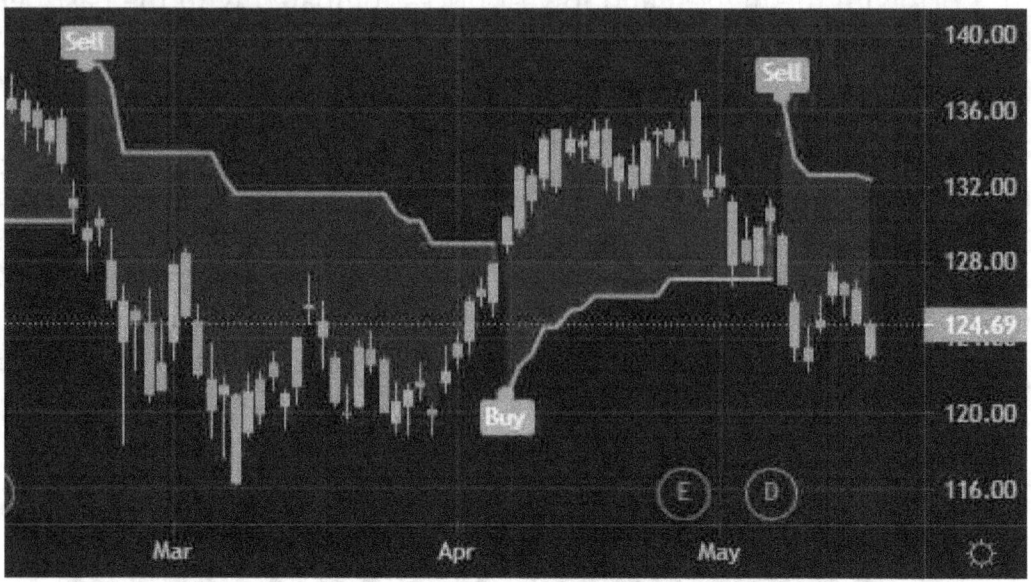

Other major built-in functions

Pivot-high and Pivot-lows

These functions allow swing traders to mark swing-high or swing-low points on the chart. Swing traders know the importance of pivot-high and low. Traders use them for marking support and resistance lines. Some traders also do trading upon breaking out any of these pivot points.

Below is the chart showing pivot-high and pivot-low points on the chart.

You can never know whether the current bar is a pivot high or low unless a few more bars are formed, and the reverse trend is confirmed. Similarly, to confirm a trend in a direction, you need a least 2-3 bars in that direction before you are sure that the trend is established.

Therefore, the syntax of pivothigh and pivotlow functions has two inputs, one is known as left strength, and another is known as right strength. These are the number of bars before which the trend can be confirmed. The syntax of pivot high and pivot low are given below:

PH_value = ta.pivothigh([source], leftbars, rightbars)

PL_value = ta.pivotlow([source], leftbars, rightbars)

The source value in the above syntax is optional, i.e. if you like, you may provide it; otherwise, there is no need. Generally, for pivothigh, high is the source and for pivotlow, low is the source. Typically, the leftbars value is 4, and the rightbars is 2.

Now, let us take an example wherein we are finding pivothigh. If PH_value = pivothigh(4,2), it can find a pivothigh, the value of high is stored in the PH_value, or otherwise, "na" is stored. Typically the series of PH_value looks as under :

PH_value	123	na	na	Na	na	na	na	126	Na
Bar	1	2	3	4	5	6	7	8	9

The PH_value is equal to "high" if it is a pivot point or is "na", i.e. nothing if it's not a pivot point.

One way to draw is by use of labels, and the script is provided below:

```
//@version=5
indicator("script25", overlay=true)
label.new(bar_index-2,pivothigh(4,2)*1.01,"high")
label.new(bar_index-2,pivotlow(4,2)*0.99,style=label.style_label_up,text="low")
```

Under the 'x' location, bar_index-2 is used; this is done to provide an offset of 2 bars. The offset is provided because the number of right bars used in the pivot high/low function is 2, and the pivot high/low is thus identified only after 2 bars. In place of the "y" location, the value obtained from the pivothigh or pivotlow function is used.

```
//@version=5
indicator("script26", overlay=true)

leftBars  = 4 //left strength
rightBars = 2 //right strength

swh = ta.pivothigh(leftBars, rightBars)
swl = ta.pivotlow(leftBars, rightBars)

swh_bool = not na(swh)
```

```
swh_bool = not na(swh)
swl_bool = not na(swl)

plotshape(swh_bool, text = "high", color = color.green,
  style = shape.triangledown, location = location.abovebar, offset = -rightBars)
plotshape(swl_bool, text = "low", color = color.red,
  style = shape.triangleup,   location = location.belowbar, offset = -rightBars)
```

The above code is for marking pivot high and pivot low points through the plotshape function. You can notice that offset = -2 is used over here. A new function, "not na()", has been used. The na() is a built-in function that gives "true" if the value inside the bracket is "na". I have used not na(), which means swh_bool is "true" if the value of swh/swl is other than "na".

The crossover and crossunder function

The crossover function is used to find the crossover between two values of two series. Generally, it generates signals upon crossover of moving averages of price, momentum, or oscillator crossover with the signal line.

The syntax of crossover is as under :

```
crossover_bool = ta.crossover(x, y)
```

The opposite of crossover is crossunder. As the name suggests, it is used to identify crossunder events. The syntax of crossunder is as under :

```
crossunder_bool = ta.crossunder(x, y)
```

Refer to script20 under "center of gravity", wherein buy and sell signals were generated on the COG line's crossover with the signal line. Here in the below script, we have implemented the same script, and on crossover/crossunder, bars have been marked.

```
//@version=5
indicator("script27",overlay=true)
cog_value=ta.cog(close,10)
cog_avg = ta.sma(cog_value,7)
crossover_buy = ta.crossover(cog_value,cog_avg)
crossover_sell = ta.crossunder(cog_value,cog_avg)
```

```
plotshape(crossover_buy,location=location.belowbar,style=shape.triangleup,text="buy"
)
plotshape(crossover_sell,location=location.abovebar,style=shape.triangledown,text="se
ll"
  ,color=color.red)
```

The result of the above script is shown below for your study:

We have directly interpreted the cog chart and have marked buy and sell signals on the chart itself. You can also combine other indicators with COG to generate buy and sell signals. An example is shown below:

Just change the condition of buy and sell as under :

crossover_buy = crossover(cog_value,cog_avg) and rsi(close,14) < 50

crossover_sell = crossunder(cog_value,cog_avg) and rsi(close,14) > 50

Barssince

The "barssince" function counts the number of bars since the provided condition becomes true. The "barssince" can be used in many ways; the syntax of barssince is as under :

```
bar_no = ta.barssince(condition)
```

Refer to script no 27 in the last example, wherein we had marked buy and sell signals based on the cog indicator and rsi. The number of buy and sell signals were not matching. We had buy signals in many cases and no sell signals. Now, looking at that problem, I want to exit any buy or sell trade entry exactly after 2 bars. This has been implemented by adding the "barssince" function to script27 as under:

```
//@version=5
indicator("script28",overlay=true)
cog_value=ta.cog(close,10)
cog_avg = ta.sma(cog_value,7)

crossover_buy = (ta.crossover(cog_value,cog_avg) and ta.rsi(close,14) < 50)
crossover_sell = (ta.crossunder(cog_value,cog_avg) and ta.rsi(close,14) > 50)

exit_buy = ta.barssince(crossover_buy)==2
exit_sell =ta.barssince(crossover_sell)==2

plotshape(crossover_buy or exit_sell,location=location.belowbar, style=
    shape.triangleup, text="buy")
plotshape(crossover_sell or exit_buy,location=location.abovebar, style=
    shape.triangledown, text="sell",color=color.red)
```

I have defined another set of variables exit_buy and exit_sell, which become true only when the buy and sell conditions have happened two bars ago. The true and false results are stored in the variables exit_buy and exit_sell and are used in the plotshape function. The resultant chart is shown below :

Buy/Sell signnals based on COG and exit after 2 bars

The valuewhen function

The valuewhen function is similar to the "barssince" function except that it does not return the number of bars since the condition becomes true, but it can provide any other value like high, low, close, and volume values. The syntax of the "valuewhen" function is as under :

Result_value = ta.valuewhen(condition, source, occurrence)

Now, take the script of the previous example, i.e. script28; I want to mark an entry as "Buy Entry" and "Sell Entry" and mark close as "Buy Close" and "Sell Close". Along with the buy/sell close, I also want to specify whether the trade was a profit/loss.

```
//@version=5
indicator("script29",overlay=true)
cog_value=ta.cog(close,10)
cog_avg = ta.sma(cog_value,7)

crossover_buy = (ta.crossover(cog_value,cog_avg) and ta.rsi(close,14) < 50)
crossover_sell = (ta.crossunder(cog_value,cog_avg) and ta.rsi(close,14) > 50)

exit_buy = ta.barssince(crossover_buy)==2
exit_sell =ta.barssince(crossover_sell)==2

plotshape(crossover_buy,location=location.belowbar,style=shape.triangleup,text="buy entry")
```

```
plotshape(crossover_sell,location=location.abovebar,style=shape.triangledown,text="sell entry",color=color.red)

tradeResult_sell = (ta.valuewhen(crossover_sell,open,1)-close) > 0 ? "profit":"loss"
if exit_sell
    label.new(bar_index,high,text="sell close "+tradeResult_sell)

tradeResult_buy = (close-ta.valuewhen(crossover_buy,open,1)) > 0 ? "profit":"loss"
if exit_buy
    label.new(bar_index,high,text="buy close "+tradeResult_buy)
```

The ta.valuewhen function has been used here to find the entry price. Another point that you may note is that valuewhen cannot be used inside a conditional statement, i.e. inside the "if...else" block; otherwise, the system may give you a warning.

I have used a label in place of plotshape; recall that plotshape does not allow variable text to be printed on the screen, so not using them.

User-Defined Functions

We have studied the building functions provided by the pinescript platform for easy coding. In some cases, you may be required to repeat code, and you would like to define and build your function for ease of coding and better readability.

The pinescript allows its coders to define their functions for multiple uses. Here, in this section, building user-defined functions are discussed.

Example Marking Doji Pattern

Doji is a pattern with an "open" price almost equal to the "close" price. These type of bars signifies indecision among traders.

As we have seen in the example of open = high[1], the value in the case of doji can never be exactly equal to close; we must take some tolerance value for its identification. Let's have a tolerance of 0.2%, then doji have "close" as under:

close < open * (1+0.002) and close > open * (1-0.002)

We all know that functions can take input from a user and provide output to a user, but it is not always true. There could be some functions that may take input but do not provide output; an example is a plot function.

Similarly, some functions could provide more than one output, for example, sar indicator, kc indicator, Bollinger band, etc. Here, we are marking doji, this takes no input, yet it checks for Doji condition and marks it when found.

A function is defined with the "=>" sign and not be confused with greater than equal. The greater than equal to mark is in pinescript is ">=" and not "=>".

The general format to define function is as under :

```
NameOfFunction(input1,input2.....) => statements
```

An example function to fine doji pattern is shown below:

```
FindDoji(open,close) => close < open * (1+0.002) and close > open * (1-0.002)
```

The above is a single-lined function that takes two inputs; one is an "open", and another is a "close" value. The result is either "true" or "false" generated by the right-side expression.

Let us improve this function by adding the ability to mark doji.

```
FindDoji() =>
    If close < open * (1+0.002) and close > open * (1-0.002)
        label.new(bar_index,high,text="Doji")
```

The above function should take two inputs, but since both inputs are built-in variables, there is no need to write them as input. The above function plots on charts and does not return any value.

A script with implementation code is presented below for your study:

```
//@version=5
indicator("script30",overlay=true)
FindDoji() =>
    if close < open * (1+0.002) and close > open * (1-0.002)
        label.new(bar_index,high,text="Doji")

FindDoji()
```

In the above code, we have first defined the function and called the function on the last line. The output generated by the function is shown on the below daily chart of Apple Inc.

Library

We have seen in the previous sections that functions make your code neat and more readable. The need for repeating code can be reduced. Functions are better for organizing code.

But you still need to copy the entire code function from the other script in your current script. What if a method can be developed wherein a function can be exported from a file already saved and imported in the present script without copying the code? This additional feature has been introduced in version 5 of pinescipt in the form of a library.

This new feature allows you to create a library code from which you can export functions for re-using them in another code file. The exported functions can be imported into other script files and can be used.

We demonstrate this feature of pinescript with an example. Suppose we want to create a new function to calculate SMA that only takes length as input, and the source is already "close".

Exporting function from a library

The library file can be created using an open tab under the pinescript editor and clicking on the "new blank library."

```
01: //@version=5
02:
03: library("mySMA")
04:
05: export mySMA(int x) =>
06:     ta.sma(close,x)
```

The above is library code; line 01 states the version of pinescript, i.e. 5. Line 03 declares that this file and script are for a "library" and not an "indicator". Under the library arguments like the title, the overlay can be added to change the behaviour of the library.

Coding is done in pinescript. You can only export functions from the library to another script. For export, you create a function under the library script, and such functions have the "export" keyword before the function's name.

In line 05, the function "mySMA" has been declared that take only one input, i.e. an integer. The function returns sma for the x period calculated on close. You may ask why "close" was not provided as input. The "close" is because an in-built variable can be accessed from any part of the code. The close is thus not indicated as another input. The new SMA function created in the above example does not require two inputs, i.e. source and length, but only length, because it calculates SMA on the "close" value of the bar.

You can save this library file in your tradingview cloud storage space. But before you can call this script for use in another file, you must publish the same. You can publish the library script "privately", i.e. only you or the one with the link can import the library. You can also publish the script "publically", i.e. anyone from the pinescript community can search and choose to use your script.

Once you have published the code, it gives you the path for the import of the script code. This link is generally in the below format:

Username/name of the library/ version of the code

For example, if I save and publish the above code with the library title "mySMA" and suppose my username is "minu", the library link for accessing the exported function would be :

```
"minu/mySMA/1"
```

Importing function from a library

Once you have published your library script as a public or a private script, you can access the function from the library script on another script using an "import" keyword. You use the import keyword and the path to the library to import all functions.

```
01: //@version=5
02: indicator("test-lib")
03: import achal/mySMA/1 as s
04: plot(s.mySMA(7))
05: plot(s.mySMA(14))
```

Another important point is that all the functions imported from a library script must be saved in an alias namespace. You can provide this alias after the pathname using the "as" keyword. The complete syntax to import the functions from a library script and store them in the alias is as under :

```
import [username/library name/version] as [alias name]
```

The alias name or "namespace" can be assumed as a container that stores information on all the functions imported from the library. For example, "ta" is a namespace for all the technical indicator functions and "math" is a namespace for all the math-related functions in pinescript. In the above example, at line no 3, the import keyword has been used for importing a library file with a library "title" named "mySMA" that we created in the previous section. All the functions inside the library file should be saved in namespace "s".

The function inside the namespace can be accessed by using a dot operator. In simpler terms, any functions stored in the namespace can be used using a dot operator. We can access our mySMA function created in the previous section by using "s.mySMA", where "s" is a namespace for all the functions obtained from the library file imported.

Chapter 11: Coding Auction Failure

I have intentionally chosen this topic as this topic is not known to newbies. This concept has emerged from the auction theory. In an auction, prices move in a particular direction till a winner is established. Suppose there is an auction, and the participants bid to win the item at an auction. Can an equity market be considered an auction market? In the olden days, brokers conducted the auction wherein traders bid for equities. Now, this is being done through electronic exchanges.

Now, you understand what an auction is! What is an auction failure? What if the auction, while continuing in one direction, suddenly stops and proceeds in the other direction? Take an example: I bid for $100 for an item, and another person bids for $101, now I also bid for $102 and other people bids for $102, but before a winner is announced, the auction is stopped or moves on to other item or another direction. A sudden reversal of the auction is a case of auction failure. There might be some more bidders willing to purchase at $103, but we did not look for them. When the price return to the level of an earlier auction failure, it tries to find other finds willing to purchase or sell at better prices. Now, if the auction again proceeds to the level of $102 of the earlier example, it will not stop here but instead will try to find other bidders at higher levels of $103 or $104.

Identification of Auction Failure (Method-1)

In the electronic bidding system where our equities are traded, this condition arises, and the price returns to the auction failure price levels to check for interested buyers or sellers who were left in earlier auction failure.

There could be various methods to identify auction failure. One of the simplest methods is to check for the following condition :

> 1. High of the present bar and previous bars are exactly equal, wherein the last bar was an upbar, and the recent bar was a down bar.
> 2. Low of the present bar and previous bar are exactly equal, wherein the last bar was a down bar, and the recent bar was a upbar.

The reaction to the price comes from the trapped traders, traders who have placed protective stop-loss orders to protect their orders. The price reactions are generally quick and require quick action to capture the profit. You can also use order-flow data to validate your trade. Alternatively, you can use any other indicator to validate the trade setup before putting your hard-earned money into the trade.

On the left is an auction failure where the high of the two bars are equal. When price revisits this level, they generally go higher than the auction failure level to find more sellers and take a quick reaction. The auction failure thus provides a short-selling opportunity.

On the right is an auction failure where the low of the two bars is equal. When prices revisit this level, they generally go lower than the auction failure level to find more buyers and take a quick reaction. The identification of auction failure has provided an opportunity to go long. It is always advisable to have these levels re-verified by another indicator or support resistance level before taking any position.

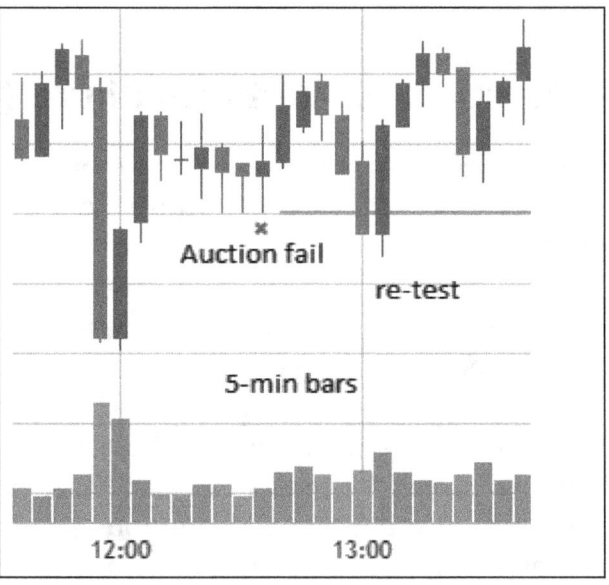

PineScript Code for Auction Failure(Method-1)

Below is the simple implementation of the Auction Failure logic. This code marks a cross above the bar that has an auction failure.

```
//@version=5
indicator("Auction Failure", overlay=true)
AuctionFailed = (high==high[1] and close < open
 and close[1] > open[1] ) or (low ==low[1] and
  close > open and close[1] < open[1]  )
plotshape(AuctionFailed)
```

The condition has two parts – 1 for finding auction failure at the highs i.e. high==high[1] and close < open and close[1] > open[1] and another is to find auction failure at the lows i.e. (low ==low[1] and close > open and close[1] < open[1]). These conditions have been joined by an "OR" logical operator.

One of them, high==high[1], becomes "true" when the high of two adjacent bars is the same. While close < open and close[1] > open[1] is to check if the first bar is a upbar and the second bar is a down bar.

The only drawback of the code is that all the marks are marked above the bar irrespective the auction failure has occurred at the lower price or the upper price. The marking problem can be resolved by adding a few extra code lines as under:

```
//@version=5
indicator("Auction Failure", overlay=true)
AuctionFailed = (high==high[1] and close < open
 and close[1] > open[1] ) or (low ==low[1] and
  close > open and close[1] < open[1]  )

plotshape(AuctionFailed and close > open ,location=location.belowbar)
plotshape(AuctionFailed and close < open ,location=location.abovebar)
```

This issue is resolved by adding two plotshape instructions with an additional location parameter. The AuctionFailed condition is combined with the upbar and down-bar conditions to have the desired result.

You would notice that more auction failures are visible in lower timeframes, and fewer are visible in higher ones.

Identification of Auction Failure (Method 2)

We notice that the auction failure are fewer on the daily timeframe chart, and the ones available in a lower timeframe provide minimal reaction. It is not feasible to capture minor reactions as the brokerage you pay is more than the reaction provided by such auction failures at a lower time frame. We need another method to identify auction failures that can give more significant reactions.

The method discussed in this book has been taken from the literature on volume profiles. I have used these as my trade setups with strict stop-loss and trail profit to earn at least 0.4% per such transaction. The stop loss is also kept at 0.4% owing to a higher winning success rate and more than 0.4% return in a few trades making these setups overall profitable. You should know there is no holy grail where you can have a trade setup with 100% winning trades. Some trades hit stop losses, but if you are earning profit at the end of the day, it is a workable setup.

I trade on 5 min timeframe chart. If you wish, you can also use 5 minute or 15 minutes time frame chart. The auction theory provides that the auction direction should not change. If the auction suddenly changes direction, the traders get trapped, or some may be willing to trade at a price level beyond the level from which the auction/ price has changed direction.

Taking the cue from the volume profile theory, the initial one hour takes traders to assess the market situation. We can safely assume that the market's direction is not decided in the first hour. After the initial first hour, the prices start moving in one direction and should continue to move in that direction till the session ends. However, from m our practical experience, we have seen that this is not true, and the price gets reversed.

In India the session starts at 9:15 am (local time) and continues till 3:30; the initial one hour ends at 10:15, and the price direction should ideally continue in one direction after 10:15 till the end of the session. However, suppose the price reverses its direction after 1:30 pm (local time) when European or other market opens. In that case, some traders are expected to get trapped in adverse positions. Other traders with winning positions would like to place stop-losses a few ticks beyond the price level from the price has reversed. So the few tick away from the price level from where the price has reversed becomes the ideal price level to provide a reaction.

But prices may take several changes in direction in a session. There could be several swing highs and lows, can all be considered auction failures?

The answer to the above question is no! Only the day's high or low beyond the initial price range of 1 hour can be considered a point of failure, provided the close is within the **initial price range of 1 hour** or on the other side of the range. Confused? Let's take an example:

PineScript Code for Auction Failure(Method-2)

```
//@version=5
indicator("Auction Failure", overlay=true)
h = request.security(syminfo.tickerid, "60", high)
l = request.security(syminfo.tickerid, "60", low)

hD = request.security(syminfo.tickerid, "D", high,lookahead=barmerge.lookahead_on)
lD = request.security(syminfo.tickerid, "D", low,lookahead=barmerge.lookahead_on)

myHigh = 0.0
myLow = 10000.00

if (hour(time) == 10 and minute(time) == 15)
   myHigh := h
   myLow  := l
else
   myHigh :=myHigh[1]
   myLow := myLow[1]

if (hour(time) == 15 and minute(time) == 15)
   myClose = close
   //find failure at highs
   if ( hD > myHigh*1.004 and myClose < myHigh)
      label.new(bar_index, hD)
   //find failure at lows
   if (lD < myLow*.996 and myClose > myLow)
      label.new(bar_index, lD)
plot(myHigh,color=color.red)
plot(myLow,color=color.red)
plot(hD)
plot(lD)
```

Below is the chart showing auction failure at the highs. You can notice that the day's high was higher than the high of the initial 4 bars of 15 mins representing 1 hour of trade. Traders somehow decided to change the direction of trade and close inside the initial range of 1-hour trade. Thus, the high point can be assumed as a point of auction failure, and trade can be taken on this.

The tradeline is drawn about 0.35% to 0.40% above the auction failure high represented on the graph, and a quick reaction of about 0.5% can be observed in the next day's trading session. A short with strict stop loss would have generated about half per cent profit.

In my experience, reaction lines are mostly broken in the first hour of volatile trade or avoided by a gap down or up. Risk-averse traders are advised not to trade in the first hour of the session as the direction of trade is not known in this first hour and may go against the above strategy.

Below is another chart showing the reaction to the auction failure.

You can notice that the reaction to the auction failure can occur after a few sessions. If the reaction is within 3-5 sessions, the reaction could be more. It depends on the number of traders trapped or stop-loss orders placed above that point. Further analysis of order flow can help you confirm the validity of trade.

?

?, 45

@

@version=4, 21

[

[ ], 34

A

alertcondition, 67
AND, 39
arithmetic operators, 38
atr, 77

B

bar_index, 92
barssince, 95
bb, 86
Boolean, 35
break, 62
Built-in Variables, 33

C

camelCase, 35
cmo, 81
cog, 82
color, 26
color.green, 26
color.red, 26
correlation, 80
crossover, 94
crossunder, 94

D

data types, 35
dmi, 89
Doji, 99

E

else if, 47
ema, 78

F

float, 35

for, 60
functions, 24

H

Historic values, 34

I

if…else, 46
iff, 40, 42
integer, 35

K

kc, 88

L

label, 54
label.delete, 63
linewidth, 26
location.abovebar, 52
location.absolute, 52
location.belowbar, 52
location.bottom, 52
location.top, 52
logical operators, 39
loop, 64

M

mfi, 83

N

NOT, 39

O

offset, 53
operators, 38
OR, 39
overlay, 20

P

parameters, 21
pivothigh, 92
pivotlow, 92
plot.style_area, 31
plot.style_circles, 31
plot.style_columns, 31
plot.style_cross, 31

plot.style_histogram, 31
plot.style_line, 31
plot.style_stepline, 31
plotchar, 51, 53
plotshape, 51

R

relational operators, 38

S

sar, 79
security, 73
shape.arrowdown, 52
shape.arrowup, 52
shape.circle, 52
shape.cross, 52
shape.diamond, 52
shape.flag, 52
shape.labeldown, 52
shape.labelup, 52
shape.square, 52
shape.triangledown, 52

shape.triangleup, 52
shape.xcross, 52
simple moving average, 23
sma, 23
stoch, 85
strategy, 20
string, 35
study, 20
supertrend, 90

T

tostring, 37, 56
type casting, 37

V

valuewhen, 97
variables, 36

W

wpr, 87

www.ingramcontent.com/pod-product-compliance
Lightning Source LLC
Chambersburg PA
CBHW080553220526
45466CB00010B/3138